Tail Risk Management

Tail Risk Management

Building A Resilient Financial Business In A Volatile World

Pascal vander Straeten

ISBN: 0692879498
ISBN 13: 9780692879498
Library of Congress Control Number: 2017908827
Value4Risk LLC, Prosper, TX

First edition: Dallas, May 2017

Strategy is born when a calculated risk meets an educated guess.
—S. Chidiac

Resilience is the quality of things that are not vulnerable to volatility.
—Anonymous

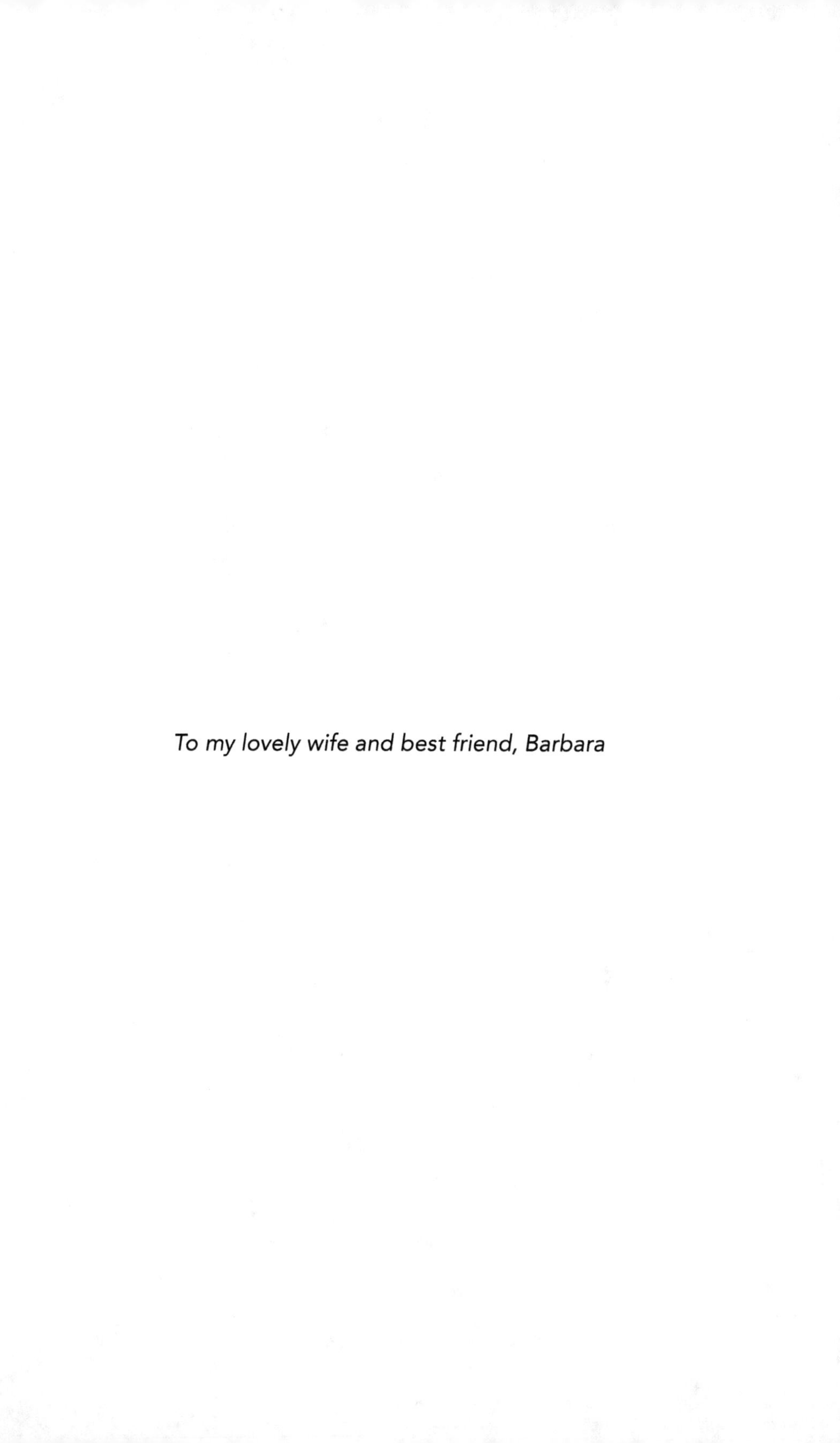

To my lovely wife and best friend, Barbara

BENEFITS OF READING THIS COMPREHENSIVE BOOK

- Prepare your financial firm for an extreme event and mitigate the impacts.
- Make sure not to become the rabbit caught in the headlights when an extreme risk affects the firm.
- Embrace volatility and uncertainty.
- Gain a holistic approach to risk management.
- Map tail risk events for financial firms.
- Build a more resilient business model.
- Explore best ways to identify, quantify, monitor, and report tail risks.
- Build a robust tail risk management system.
- Understand the interaction between financial markets, the business world, and geopolitics.
- Understand how tail risk management is much more forward looking than Basel III.

PREREQUISITES

Some prior knowledge and experience in financial risk management

A working knowledge of lending and investment practices

A basic understanding of leading approaches to Basel II and Basel III

About the Author

People who know him best say that he is a risk taker with a strong passion for financial risk, tail events, and geopolitics. During his global career, Pascal advanced through a number of risk-management assignments, having covered institutional banking, corporate banking, project finance, public finance, commercial real estate, structured finance, and emerging markets with successful missions in the United States, the United Kingdom, Germany, Italy, Spain, France, Luxembourg, and Belgium. In 2012, together with his family, he moved to Australia, where he established his own company—Value4Risk—and secured talks and speaking engagements on tail risk management in an academic and professional setting with exposure to business entrepreneurs. Today, he is also present in the United States, pursuing the same activities. He holds an executive MBA from the University of Washington, a postgraduate in international relations from the Université Catholique de Louvain, and a master's in applied economics from the University of Antwerpen.

Why Should You Read This Book?

Remember the famous quote from Donald Rumsfeld in 2002: "There are known knowns; there are things we know we know. We also know there are known unknowns; that is to say we know there are some things that we do not know. But there are also unknown unknowns—the ones we don't know we don't know."

Everyone will acknowledge that capital (equity) is the primary and ultimate driver of defense against unexpected losses from unquantifiable uncertainty. As a result, the objective of managing unquantifiable uncertainty is to preserve and protect capital from extreme risks. But risk management and tail risk management have such different objectives and motivations that one cannot be merely extended to manage the other.

Traditional risk management drives a firm's revenue engine, while tail risk management preserves the firm's survivability (but bear in mind that tail risk management is more than just capital management). Therefore, relying on traditional risk management to manage just-in-case risks (or extreme financial risk) is a disaster waiting to happen, as shown by the events of 2008.

The massive failures among large and respected financial institutions over the last ten years, particularly during the global financial crisis, clearly illustrate that current risk management practices and banking regulations fail to provide adequate responses to the challenges set by tail risks.

The recent global financial crisis (GFC) has highlighted that seemingly sound balance sheet fundamentals (such as strong capital and liquidity) do not always suffice to shield financial firms from a systemic crisis, and that effective tail risk management can lead to building a more resilient business model. But concomitantly this business resiliency requires a real change in management in terms of governance and business practices, failing which the firm's risk architecture will not be appropriately tailored to face extreme events. While the context of this book is financial services, the chapters contain important takeaway messages for many other businesses active in any industries exposed to extreme risks (oil/gas, energy, mining, chemicals productions, transportation, etc.).

This book will show you how tail risk management is very different from traditional risk management in the sense that instead of relying on probability theories, extreme risks should be addressed through the prism of business resiliency. Therefore, this book will focus much more on the governance, architecture, qualitative methods, and risk mitigation techniques surrounding tail risk management than on the quantitative approaches, such as hedging.

The interesting feature about this book is the fact that many concepts used to address tail risk events and business resiliency have been borrowed from the nonbanking world. For example, supply chain risk management is used in the manufacturing world, while threat assessment has been borrowed from disaster recovery agencies (FEMA in the United States). The concept of high-reliability organizations is implemented in the health-care services industry, and probable maximum loss is a metric used in the insurance industry.

As such, the author has tried to be creative and open-minded in looking at the best market practices across industries to address tail risk events and business resiliency. This book does not claim to cover the management of extreme risks exhaustively; however, it could be used as an appetizer or a platform to further dig into those concepts.

It is also key to note that this book has found inspiration and grounds for further research through many other books that have equally addressed the topic of the risk management of extreme events. Therefore, the author has attempted to consolidate these existing essays on tail risk management and bring their findings to the attention of firms active in the financial services industry. For the sake of academic accountability, the author has, as much as he could, referenced each and every work he consulted or cited.

A last but not trivial remark: you will notice that in several passages of this book, several concepts and statements are being repeated. It's on purpose, and the reason is twofold:

- Repeat for clarity: Like it or not, many readers skim. No matter how clearly concepts are expressed the first time, these words may literally not have been seen. Content needs to cut through a reader's dense fog of information clutter, chronic interruption, and recurring fantasies about such things as risk management, probabilities, extreme risks, and black swans. And since many concepts are important, they are worth repeating. It's especially important to repeat calls to action.
- Repeat for certainty: Don't assume readers got it the first time or that they still remember it. Since this book contains some powerful or important ideas, the audience is being hit with them more than once. Whether the concepts are being spoken to new readers or old hands, it makes sense to repeat key messages every few chapters or so. The more you repeat a concept, the deeper and richer the thinking gets each time the concept is revisited.

Contents

Introduction

This book is primarily the result of a passion that combines financial risk management, extreme risks, geopolitics, and strategic management. It took me many years to write this book, not only because I was working on it on and off but also because it took a lot of research. If you go to my LinkedIn page, you will find many of these topics in the more than four hundred articles I have posted. I am fully aware that the work is not exhaustive, because like any research, a work is never completed. As the Greek philosopher Aristotle once said, "The more you know, the more you know you don't know."

What brought me to the idea of this book was the onset of the global financial crisis that hit the United States and the rest of the world back in 2007–2008. When that crisis took place, I kept on hearing "We never expected it," "It totally came as a surprise," or "This is something that no one could ever have predicted."

Today, many claim the world is much more erratic and volatile than it was thirty years ago, and, given the nonlinear environment in which we are living, it is very difficult to forecast disruptive events. In other words, we can expect another crisis lurking behind the corner.

Other people claim that history is merely repeating itself, and it is a feeling of déjà vu. A clear understanding of extreme risks should guide any reasonable approach to managing financial and business risk, yet the two most widely used measures in financial firms today—probability and value at risk (VaR)—attempt to reduce these risks to single digits, creating a false sense of security among risk managers, executives, and regulators.

This book introduces a more realistic and holistic framework, drawing from existing market practices in the corporate world, such as supply chain risk management and sustainable business models, that enable one to conceptualize the different kinds of financial and business risks and to design effective strategies for managing them.

Instead of focusing solely on quantitative risk management, I want to emphasize aspects of qualitative risk management, combining more robust business continuity and control procedures with organizational management supported by stronger governance and risk awareness. This is undoubtedly a somewhat idiosyncratic description of the role of tail risk management (TRM) in making both financial and business decisions.

But this focus on risk management to help build a more resilient financial firm rests on the fact that it is the aspect of the process I believe I know best. More importantly, TRM is at the nexus between decision makers and the vast risk management apparatus, and the aim of TRM is to reduce uncertainty and reinforce business resiliency by providing insightful information tailored to the specific needs of a vast array of stakeholders, such as portfolio managers, risk managers, senior executives, business development managers, entrepreneurs, investors, regulators, and a myriad of others.

Over the years of my professional life, I have had opportunities to interact directly with many such stakeholders at many levels. What I have learned is that overreliance on mathematical (financial) models is a recipe for disaster. Indeed, underestimated volatility and imperfect model assumptions may lead to a wrong outcome.

While algebra has increasingly become important in mathematical research and its applications, and imposing a logical consistency on thinking has proved to be largely beneficial, caution needs to be exercised. Indeed, the problem is the illusion that mathematical models create, namely, that the knowledge of the peak of the iceberg could be generalized to the remainder of the submerged iceberg. With the intensive use of computers in combination with big data, algebraic statements are like a kind of coding: precise and logical. But while mathematical models can replicate a lot, they cannot replicate past events that did not occur in large numbers.

Therefore, this book will mostly focus on the qualitative process involving TRM and not so much on hedging and other quantitative techniques. I do believe risk management is much more than merely hedging and quantitative analysis, as so well stated through this definition: "The systematic application of management policies, procedures and practices to the tasks of establishing the context, identifying, analyzing, assessing, treating, monitoring and communicating."[1]

Thus, I will focus on qualitative risk management processes, such as risk mapping, scenario building, reverse stress testing, early warning, supply chain risk management and resiliency, financial continuity planning (FCP), mutualizing risk resources, behavioral risk management, and building more resilient business models.

Ever since the 1990s, and particularly in the aftermath of the global financial crisis (GFC) with the promulgation of Basel III, the financial services industry has spent hundreds of millions of dollars in setting compliance and risk management frameworks, IT risk infrastructure, and so on, to reduce uncertainty by attempting to forecast the next financial or economic crisis and shield financial firms from unexpected losses. Virtually every risk management department in any financial firm monitors and forecasts a wide range of developments through mathematical models and risk measurement techniques.

But many organizations remain insufficiently prepared for potential crises—even eight years after the GFC. Here, one should clarify what causes a crisis: it is a significant disruption that totally overhauls a previous

1 "Risk Management Process, Biological Risk Assessment Group," University of Arkansas, accessed February 2, 2017, http://www.uark.edu/ua/biorisk/education/more_definitions.pdf.

set of assumptions and ways of going about business, bringing with it new and often unknown threats, chaos, and uncertainty. It has major and lasting consequences that call into question the stability of the organization suffering the crisis, thus necessitating rapid decision making. This means, then, that "routine" disturbances, failures, and incidents do not invoke resilience, since they are controlled by the existing processes that are driving the way how business is usually being done.

Now, when a crisis does hit, companies typically struggle to get back up and running. If your own organization were to be struck by a significant crisis tomorrow, how resilient would it be? Would you merely survive the emergency, or would you come through it as strong as you are today (or maybe even stronger)?

So in the aftermath of the GFC, not to mention the current lingering euro debt showdown, this book on TRM attempts to answer the question, "What changes should financial institutions undergo to ensure reliable protection against low-probability, high-severity risks?"

Through this book, I will combine an analysis of the nature of tail risk (so-called extreme risk), risk management practices, and practical solutions to build a robust, enterprise-wide, extreme risk management framework, which includes three lines of defense, ranging from strategic to tactical, designed to help address tail risk during different stages of its development.

Additionally, I will try to answer

(i) why modern "sophisticated" risk management frameworks, strong capitalization, and liquidity do not prevent financial firms from failing in the face of systemic crisis;
(ii) what it means to build an effective tail risk defense against systemic and catastrophic losses;
(iii) what risk architecture should look like to ensure extreme risk events are identified early and efficiently mitigated; and
(iv) how modern management practices, regulations, and risk and business culture need to change to guarantee sustainability. While

the context is financial services, the work contains important take-away messages for businesses active in any industry exposed to extreme risks (e.g., oil/gas, energy, mining, chemical productions, transportation).

Tail Events—Scope

How Tail Risks Affect Businesses

Tail risk is usually discussed in the scope of portfolio investments and financial hedging strategies; however, the nonfinancial world is also vulnerable to tail risk. The objective of this book is first and foremost to help create awareness among the executive leadership of financial firms (but also among business entrepreneurs in the nonfinancial world) that tail risk does affect their income decisions and that strategies do exist to mitigate it.

Tail risks affect business decisions as risk-averse entrepreneurs, who differ in their known skills and who face idiosyncratic efficiency risk, make investment and business income decisions. Depending on the development stage of the firm, entrepreneurs can diversify or not. The upside and downside risks are illustrated by the fatness of the right and left tails of the bell-shaped normal distribution curve that represents the business income risk. Global interconnectivity makes companies more reliant than ever on other businesses and markets. Information today is disseminated and processed faster than ever before, ironically leaving management with a reduced window to respond to an incident.

No entrepreneur or board member wants his or her company to experience the fate of MF Global, Enron, Worldcom, AIG, Bear Stearns, or Lehman Brothers. Therefore, minimizing exposure to sudden catastrophic events—known academically as extreme tail risks—must be a top priority for executive boards because of their devastating financial impact.

As entrepreneurs and board members seek to better shield their businesses from these threats, they should remember that risk has two distinct dimensions: one, when managed effectively, drives the revenue engine; the other, if not managed effectively, threatens financial havoc in the event of a large crisis. Companies have historically used conventional risk management to provide oversight for the former; however, companies also need to manage the latter dimension—low-probability extreme risk—but not as a mere extension of the traditional risk management discipline. Failure to do this can be a recipe for disaster, not only as the objectives are starkly different but also because traditional risk management tools cannot even measure these critical threats objectively.

That is why, during the GFC in 2008, well-known financial institutions such as Washington Mutual, Lehman Brothers, and Bear Stearns were caught by total surprise when their business models abruptly failed.

So how can boards ensure that their companies do not operate too close to the edge and become unwitting victims of "too much extreme risk"? According to Paul Karamjeet et al. (2014), three changes are needed:

√ First, a board must recognize that a company will fail not because it has too much risk but because it has too much extreme risk. This distinction is critical, because in a first step, tail risks need to be identified and mapped. For Paul Karamjeet (2014), traditional risk management is based on the theory of probability, where the cost of being wrong is the loss of profits. However, with so-called tail risk, the cost of being wrong can be deadly for companies. Traditional risk management foresees that things will go awry and provides for solutions. With tail risk, it is mostly assumed that there is no telling how a catastrophic event can arise, as experienced by Swissair, Polaroid, PanAm, Enron, LTCM, or BP in the *Deepwater Horizon* disaster, although later in the book, I will highlight that tail risks are often the result of strategic mistakes. Karamjeet rightly points out that since the company's survival could be at stake, it is dysfunctional to address a company's sustainability using the classic drivers of traditional risk management, such as probabilities and expected values. Obviously, a new approach is needed.

√ Second, tail risk requires metrics to quantify it so it can be addressed effectively. Boards and companies use precisely defined measures, such as earnings, profitability, and volatility, to manage their businesses. Should there not be one for extreme risk too? The complexities of today's revenue models make it paramount that tail risk be measured distinctly, transparently, and simply so that effective oversight can be established. Many mathematical models that do exist claim that they can measure tail risks, such as the conditional value-at-risk (CoVaR), expected shortfall (ES), and extreme value theory (EVT). The insurance industry's commonly used concept of a "probable maximum loss" (PML) model can also be an effective tool for extreme risk management. This approach can capture extreme risk continuously at financial and industrial companies alike so that they can avoid being blindsided in crises. However, I opt for a more qualitative approach using risk mapping, reverse stress testing, supply chain risk management, scenario planning, and other methods to identify where in a firm's process and organization extreme risks are stored.

√ Third, companies need sound policies and procedures to diligently manage and mitigate tail risks. This must start with the distinct board oversight of how much tail risk is too much and what limitations and governance are needed specifically for its effective management. Boards can address the extreme risk problem only if they create a company-wide culture of awareness that identifies potential sources of future tail risks, establish specific risk monitoring processes that include nontraditional threats, and fully integrate risk not only into the business strategies and decision making but also into the finance/treasury department, as much of the information will need to be shared between these areas. These steps need to be formalized by means of guidelines. But foremost, boards need a financial contingency plan that should be looked at more broadly than the well-business contingency plan.

By adopting the three steps above, boards can help ensure their company's future survival.

What Are Tail Events?

DEFINITION OF A TAIL EVENT

Occasionally, some event occurs that no one expected. A tail event is a product that, from the perspective of the regularity of historical events or perhaps only from perception, should happen only once in a thousand, million, or billion years. Significant tail events include the dropping of the first nuclear bombs over Nagasaki and Hiroshima in 1945; the Korean War in 1950–1953; the Six-Day War in 1967; the sharp rise in oil prices in 1973; the Iranian Revolution in 1979; the 23 percent fall in stock prices on October 19, 1987; the destruction of the World Trade Center twin towers in 2001; the global financial crisis in 2007–2008; and the Greek debt crisis in 2009–2010.

TAIL EVENTS IN THE STATISTICAL WORLD

Tail events in the statistical realm can be defined as low-probability, high-severity events that can dominate the impacts and "societal concerns for many issues, of which climate change is a signal example. This is the problem known as 'fat tails.[2] To illustrate the problem of fat tails, it is helpful to first picture a probability distribution such as the common bell curve or normal distribution. The normal distribution has most observations clustering around the center, with few showing highly divergent results.

2 W. Nordhaus, "Elementary Statistics of Tail Events," paper, Yale University, April 8, 2011.

Tail Events in Literature: Black Swans

Tail events in the literature are commonly known as black swans. Indeed, the black swan theory is a metaphor describing an event that comes as a surprise, has a major effect, and is often inappropriately rationalized after the fact with the benefit of hindsight.

The term *black swan* has recently been popularized through the book written by Nassim Nicholas Taleb (2007), *The Black Swan*. Taleb's definition of a black swan is neat, as it rests on three main attributes: the event (1) should be an outlier, (2) should have an extreme impact, and (3) could, in hindsight, be rationalized. A black swan is exactly that; it is a tail or extreme risk event that no one really expected, but as it took place, it had a disastrous impact on its environment.

As already mentioned, Taleb (2007) developed the theory to explain[3]:

- "The disproportionate role of high-profile, hard-to-predict, and rare events that are beyond the realm of normal expectations in history, science, finance, and technology.
- "The non-computability of the probability of the consequential rare events using scientific methods (owing to the very nature of small probabilities).
- "The psychological biases that blind people, both individually and collectively, to uncertainty and to the massive role of rare events in historical affairs."

Obviously, Taleb was not the first to popularize the term *black swan*. In the eighteenth century, David Hume (1777),[4] through his theory of inductive reasoning, questioned whether giving credence to the properties of a particular class of objects based on some limited number of observations of particular instances of that class (e.g., the inference that "all swans we have seen are white; therefore, all swans are white," before the discovery

3 *Wikipedia*, s.v. "Black Swan Theory," https://en.wikipedia.org/wiki/Black_swan_theory.

4 D. Hume, *An Enquiry Concerning Human Understanding* (Salt Lake City: Gutenberg Press, #9662, 1902), last modified October 16, 2007.

of black swans) would necessarily lead to the ultimate truth, or in other words whether one could extrapolate a general observation from a limited sample of observations. An additional example is presupposing that a sequence of events in the future will occur as it always has in the past (e.g., that the laws of physics will hold, as they have always been observed to hold). Hume called this the principle of uniformity of nature. Way before Hume, there was Sextus Empiricus (AD 160), who questioned the validity of inductive reasoning, positing that a universal rule could not be established from an incomplete set of instances.[5] In more modern times, Karl Popper also juggled with the term *black swan* by trying to solve the problem of induction.[6] Popper held that seeking theories with a high probability of being true is a false goal that conflicts with the search for knowledge. Science should seek theories that, on the one hand, are probably false (which is the same as saying they are highly falsifiable, and so there are many ways they could turn out to be wrong), but that, on the other hand, have had all actual attempts to falsify them fail so far (they are highly corroborated).

UNDERSTANDING THE DIFFERENCE BETWEEN RISK AND UNCERTAINTY

Risk and uncertainty are really two ends of a single spectrum; that is, either you know the probability, or you do not know the probability.

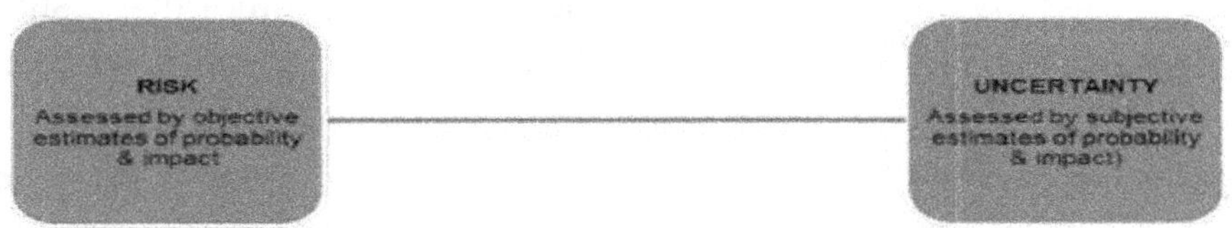

From Knight, Ellsberg, and Kahneman, "Project Risk Management Incorporating."[7]

5 Sextus Empiricus, *Outlines of Pyrrhonism*, trans. Robert Gregg Bury (Loeb ed.) (London: W. Heinemann, 1933), 283.

6 K. Popper, *The Logic of Scientific Discovery* (London: Hutchinson & Co., 1959).

7 J. Prpić, *Project Risk Management Incorporating* paper (Kauai: IEEE Computer Society Press, 2016), last revised April 11, 2016.

As such, risk is different from uncertainty, according to the great economist Frank Knight (1921). He used risk to describe cases of known probability, while uncertainty, according to Knight, is when one faces unknown probabilities.

It is worthwhile to understand the difference between uncertainty and risk, and to relate this to industry applications:

- Risk: We do not know what will happen next, but we do know what the distribution looks like.
- Uncertainty: We do not know what will happen next, and we do not know what the possible distribution looks like.

The future is always unknown, but that does not make it uncertain. John Maynard Keynes used the example of a company considering an investment in a copper smelter, which could last years and years. The company has no accurate idea regarding what the price of copper will be in twenty to thirty years, nor is it certain what will be the probability of different possible prices.

When you apply this concept to, for instance, supply chains in the corporate world, enterprises know that having a supply chain almost always involves a certain amount of risk. However, few do enough to protect against the one-off, extreme incidents that can disrupt them. Such events, sometimes referred to as *black swans*, include unanticipated catastrophes, such as Hurricane Katrina, the BP *Deepwater Horizon* oil rig explosion, the 9/11 terrorist attack, the tsunami that hit Japan in 2011, and even the Volkswagen emissions scandal.

While most risk planning processes focus on events that happen relatively often, such as routine weather emergencies, they often ignore the extreme cases considered too unlikely to worry about. Although such events are unlikely, the probability they will take place is not zero, as history has repeatedly proved. Black swans are never expected. There are many examples of low-probability, high-impact disruptions. People do not believe they can happen, but they do—and there will be more.

However, it is not easy to connect all the dots. A large company can have several hundreds of suppliers and contractors, for instance, and each of those third parties may have subsuppliers of their own. With all those moving parts, managing all the places disaster can strike is a complex matter.

CONFUSION BETWEEN CRASH, VOLATILITY, AND TAIL EVENTS

Given the recent financial turmoil in 2008, the study of tail events has become a central preoccupation for academics, investors, and policymakers alike. But what differentiates a crash from a tail event?

A study by Sofiane Aboura (2012) highlights that it is easy to become confused about crash and tail events. She used an augmented extreme value theory approach. The extreme value theory has widely documented ways in which extreme events can be quantified. According to Aboura, in order to be labeled as a crash, it has to have three attributes: (1) a sudden event causing (2) a significant decline on (3) a one-day horizon.

With the latter in mind, she argues that it is almost impossible to hedge a portfolio against a crash within a period of one day or less. A tail event is not the result of a sudden event, as a crash would be, but instead the fruit of a long period of volatility. In other words, if a business is in a period of high volatility, the occurrence of a tail risk is much higher than if the same firm is in a low-volatility environment. Volatility represents the level of uncertainty about the markets or the economic backdrop of which the markets are a part.

This correlation between volatility and tail risk has been explicated through new statistics called conditional kurtosis and conditional skewness. In essence, kurtosis (i.e., the shape of a probability distribution) and skewness (i.e., a measure of the asymmetry of the probability distribution) are statistics used to determine how far a distribution deviates from the normal distribution. The term *conditional* here is used in the Bayesian sense of the term. Namely, Bayes's theorem answers the question: "What is the probability of event A given that event B has occurred?" Here we are asking "What is the kurtosis (or tail risk) given that we are in a high (or low) uncertainty environment?" In high uncertainty, kurtosis is a high positive number with a high level of significance showing that the tail is much fatter than the normal distribution. By contrast, the low-uncertainty kurtosis is also significant, but kurtosis is negative, meaning that the tails are thinner than those of the normal distribution.

Are Tail Events Really Unknown Unknowns?

KNOWN UNKNOWNS AND UNKNOWN UNKNOWNS

There is a very interesting book written by Diebold, Doherty, and Herring (2010) that provides a clear understanding of what we know, do not know, and cannot know, which should guide any reasonable approach to managing financial risks. These comprise the following:

- There are known knowns. There are things we know that we know.
- There are known unknowns. There are things that we know we do not know.
- There are also unknown unknowns. There are things we do not know that we do not know.

The interesting part about this understanding is that over time the gradual recognition of previously unknown unknowns leads to the proliferation of a family of known unknowns, which can then be tackled by traditional hypothesis forming and testing, occasionally discovering another unknown unknown, and so the cycle continues. In other words, over time, unknown unknowns tend to become known unknowns and eventually even known knowns as science progresses.

CAUSES OF TAIL EVENTS

Evgueni Ivantsov (2013) has written an excellent book about tail risks ("Heads or Tails: Financial Disaster, Risk Management and Survival Strategy in the World of Extreme Risk"), and he examines how these extreme events take place. His findings show that four of the most standard causes of tail risks are the following:

1. The phenomenon of unknown unknowns relatively rarely triggers tail risk events. Many events simply are without precedent, undercutting the basis of this type of reasoning altogether. It can only relate to very new financial instruments (e.g., exotic derivatives) of which the behavior could be less known to market participants.
2. Many extreme events in different areas of human activity have been triggered by coincidence of multiple noncritical errors. Ivantsov cites a relatively recent example in the financial world: the June 12, 2012, failure of the Royal Bank of Scotland's payment system, which led to around 750,000 bank customers being unable to use their credit and debit cards.
3. Reckless behavior was and remains the source of many extreme events. An accident can be triggered by a deliberate human error. Ivantsov illustrates this by referring to the Chernobyl disaster (April 24, 1986) caused by operators breaking the operation rules. In the financial industry, the most notorious examples of such extreme-event causes are cases of "rogue" trading or large-scale frauds (e.g., Nick Leeson and Barings Bank in 1992, Bernard Madoff and the Ponzi scheme in 2008, and Jérôme Kerviel and Société Générale in 2008).
4. Strategic mistakes are often the primary causes of tail risk events; yet it is difficult to spot these errors, and for many years they remain under cover until, by coincidence, these mistakes become apparent. Ivantsov showcases this by flagging the Fukushima Daiichi nuclear disaster (Ōkuma, Fukushima, Japan, in 2011), the second-largest nuclear accident after Chernobyl (also Level 7 on

> the International Nuclear Radiological Event Scale). Indeed, the event reveals a case in which a strategic mistake triggered a failure of crucial systems, which in turn led to an extreme disaster (on March 11, 2011, the plant was hit by a tsunami, and the subsequent failure of the emergency cooling system caused the explosion). The fundamental cause of the accident was a string of strategic mistakes in both the plant location and its design.

However you look at it, unfortunately, strategic blunders are the most common cause of extreme events in the financial sector and, most likely, in the nonfinancial sector. What does this tell us? These extreme events are usually steered by human factors driven by greed, ego, grandeur, and so on.

There is no such thing as an invisible hand that would put a grain of sand in our complex machines. Rather, humans are the cause of all evil. As already illustrated through the abovementioned examples, many notorious failures came as a direct result of strategic mistakes made in the financial services industry by the firm's senior executive leadership teams (e.g., UBS, AIG, Northern Rock, HBOS, RBS, Dexia, Financial Assured Guarantee, and Wachovia). In the case of the nonfinancial industry, Enron, WorldCom, Swissair, Polaroid, Commodore Computers, and Pan Am resulted from wrong strategic decisions or bad incidents.

This categorization of the four key underlying causes of extreme risk events not only helps us better comprehend the nature of tail risk but also provides us with clues on how we can prevent extreme risk events going forward. Only the first category—cases stemming from unknown unknowns—is entirely unavoidable.

However, even for unknown unknowns, I honestly have my doubts. For example, in the case of exotic collateralized debt obligations (CDOs) or credit default swaps (CDSs), one must know that sooner or later, this scheme of selling toxic assets through highly rated debt is bound to fall apart. The Ponzi scheme went on because the market supporting these subprime assets remained bullish (and rating agencies were corrupted in pretending that senior tranches in these investment vehicles were safe investments), but once the trend became bearish, the whole scheme collapsed. Therefore, here too I would say that the human factor (greed, ego, and complacency) played a big role.

As for the other three categories, they are truly preventable. As Ivantsov (2013) mentioned:

> Errors and failures of different elements of the system (isolated or simultaneous) are definitely preventable. Human reckless behavior and the violation of the existing rules and common sense can also and must be preventable via the strict governance and comprehensive control of all key activities that have extreme risk-linked exposure.

Granted, we cannot fully protect ourselves from threats that we do not know about; however, we can instead try to protect ourselves from harm caused by, for instance, cases of bad leadership decisions. Therefore, one could state that tail risks are not always an unavoidable evil. It is true that, when people deliberately abuse the system, it may take years before these mistakes become known. Additionally, if the leadership team leads with a bad example, quite possibly staff will mimic this wrong behavior. For example, look at the recent scandal regarding retail banking practices at Wells Fargo in early 2017 in which aggressive sales incentives and business culture pushed employees into defrauding customers by opening accounts and buying products they had not requested. That is why, for people inside the organization, it is almost impossible to spot the strategic error well before it triggers the extreme event.

TAIL EVENTS AND UNEXPECTED LOSSES

Since the 1980s, the Basel regulation has developed an approach to calculate the economic capital needed to absorb losses caused by events for which the probability is difficult to estimate.[8] In practice, in the finan-

8 The Basel regime is an international system of capital adequacy regulation designed to strengthen banks' financial health as well as the safety and soundness of

cial world, economic capital approaches use a model based on the value at risk (VaR). Within the prudential framework, economic capital should provide compensation for unexpected and unanticipated losses that are being accounted for when financial institutions are compelled to function outside their normal operating environment.

To estimate economic capital, the VaR model essentially breaks the return distribution down into two segments: a likely expected loss and an unlikely unexpected loss. Unexpected loss is estimated by setting an extremely high threshold (unlikely probability). The difference between unexpected and expected loss serves as an estimate for economic capital.

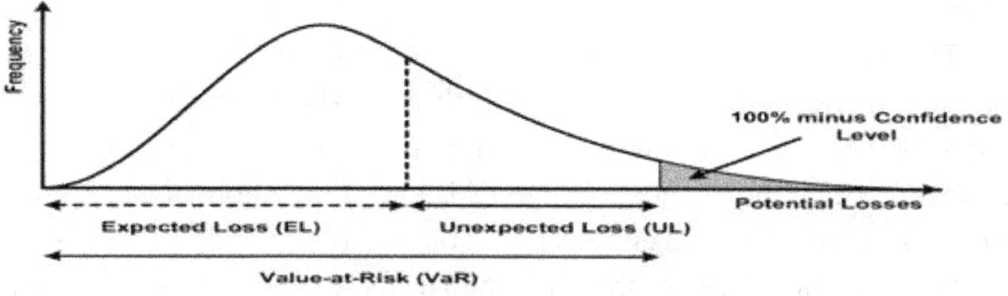

From the Center for Safety Research, Department of Transport Science, KTH Royal Institute of Technology.[9]

The typical loss profile from financial risk contains occasional extreme losses among frequent events of low-loss severity. Firms categorize operational risk losses as expected losses, which are absorbed by net profit, and unexpected losses, which are covered by risk reserves through core capital or hedging. The expected loss represents a loss that arises from the daily business, while the unexpected loss is the number of standard deviations away from the expected loss (the tail of the distribution).

---

the financial system. It originated with the 1988 Basel Accord, now known as Basel I, and was then overhauled. Basel II had still not been implemented in the United States when the financial crisis struck in 2008, and in the wake of the banking system collapse, regulators rushed out Basel III.

9 D. Gorton, "Aspects of Modeling Fraud Prevention of Online Financial Services" (Doctoral thesis, KTH Royal Institute of Technology, Stockholm, Sweden, 2015).

Expected losses are typically covered through ratings as well as loss given default (provisions), while unexpected losses are merely covered by capital. While firms should generate enough expected revenues to support a net margin after accounting for the expected component of financial risk from predictable failures and defaults, they also need to provide sufficient economic capital to cover the unexpected component.

The unexpected loss is calibrated at, for example, the 99.95 percent confidence level, which from a rating perspective corresponds to an "AA" rating, meaning in practice this is variously expressed as a risk of defaulting once in two thousand years or, alternatively, as one in two thousand AA-rated banks defaulting in any given year. Obviously, this is based on statistics that are mirror-based and not forward looking.

Therefore, financial firms calibrate their economic capital models according to management's risk appetite, which is usually in line with the firm's target rating. Where the financial institutions still get it wrong on unexpected losses is that the confidence interval is based on a normal distribution, whereas extreme (tail risk) events are not based on a normal distribution.

Subsequently, they use that system to calibrate their business model in such a way as to reach, for example, an AA rating (still under a normal distribution with a couple of standard deviations from the average). Economic capital is set based on high-probability events, while it should also encompass low-probability, high-severity events mirrored by the recent GFC, the upcoming deflation scenario in Europe, or the collapse of China's house of cards. Under the current existing economic capital rules, unexpected losses are measured by the variability around expected losses.

Moreover, as Moody's KMV states, "The level of economic capital implies a probability of capital exhaustion and an associated debt rating. Given the portfolio loss distribution and a target debt rating, the required economic capital may be inferred."[10]

---

10 B. Dvorak, *Uses and Misuses of Required Economic Capital* (New York: Moody's KMV Company, 2005).

HOW TO DEAL WITH UNKNOWNS?

The known unknowns and unknown unknowns in an organization differ from person to person. Getting people together to share information and make joint decisions is the best way to deal with the unknown. Typically, highly reliable organizations (such as in the health-care sector or the chemicals industry) use this system of information sharing and communication in order to better deal with unexpected events.

Thus, the key is to identify tail events as a specific risk domain, collect and share information about it, and develop collective decisions and actions. Many of the risky events seem beyond the control of senior leadership who are attempting to shield their businesses in an unstable political-economic environment:

- √ Hackers and other cybercriminals pose threats to governments as well as businesses.
- √ The debt crises in Europe and in China affect businesses worldwide and the entire global economy.
- √ The election results in the United States will lead to a change in the geopolitical environment, whether for the better or worse.
- √ Natural cataclysms pose a threat to supply chains that are often spread across the globe.

However, tactics and tools do exist to help businesses and organizations survive and thrive despite these threats—in other words, to make them more resilient. The key is to first look inward by examining the most vulnerable points within the organization, distinguishing between core competencies (and business lines) and those that are not, determining the business's points of stress in terms of finance and capital, and determining what assumptions are made in the business. That is the philosophy of how we perceive these unknowns.

I propose several emerging strategies for coping with these unknowns (borrowed from best market practices across industries):

1. Risk mapping: List the core activities and distinguish them from any side businesses. This will allow one to focus on the core skills and businesses.
2. Reverse stress testing: For example, to identify vulnerabilities, start from a failure scenario and work backward to see how serious a recession would sink the business.
3. Scenario planning: This may include building buffers to absorb shock and may be a reason so many companies now sit on significant quantities of cash. Thus, determine where the cash is, what will happen to it, the current liabilities (including off-balance-sheet items), and what will happen to the cash flow.
4. Supply chain risk management (part of a dedicated TRM strategy): Situating enterprise risk management (ERM) responsibility within the strategy group may be an emerging best practice, as long as it interacts closely with the various business lines. In other words, build risk management within the existing management processes.
5. Financial continuity planning (a way to respond to emerging threats): Firm-wide integration of IT and financial systems, as well as mutualization of resources, can help companies respond to risk events.

Each of these strategies (and a couple of others)—aimed at making a business model more resilient—will be further discussed in the following chapters.

Tail Risk Management: Definition and Governance

Why We Are Running the Risk of Wasting a Good Crisis

FINDINGS OF ALLIANZ GLOBAL INVESTORS RISK MONITOR 2016 SURVEY[11]

Tail risk has become a recurring topic of discussion since 2008, when investors were painfully reminded that unpredictable events carrying the potential for major market disruption occur more frequently than normal bell curves (which traditional portfolio construction strategies rely on) would have us believe. Tail events in the market are more common than perhaps historically anticipated, which is a huge problem for investors.

> Tail risk describes the type of market shocks that are not generally expected, but since the financial crisis, institutional investors have become increasingly wary of these potentially cataclysmic events. The question of whether a tail risk event is looming provokes a difference of opinion among investors. A considerable number (37%) globally believe a tail risk event is likely to take place in the next 12 months. This view is however countered by the more positive 33% who think this is unlikely.

---

11 Allianz Global Investors Risk Monitor, Global Edition 2016. Risk Monitor helps to raise awareness about the trials and tribulations that institutional investors face across the globe.

Concern is highest in the Americas (41%) followed by the EMEA region (38%). Institutional investors in Asia-Pacific are the least worried about a potential tail risk event, with 33% expressing concern.[12]

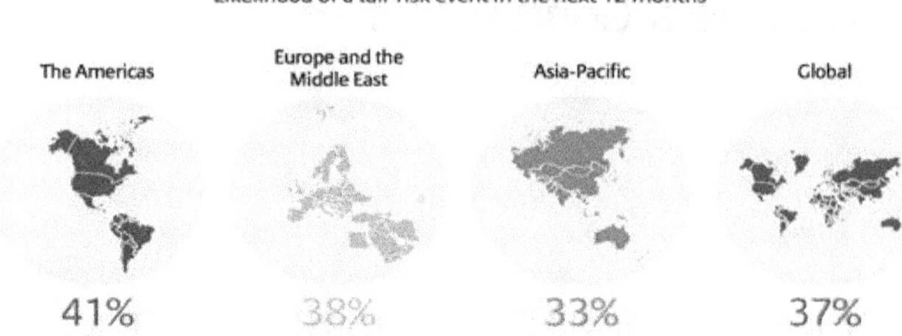

From Allianz Global Investors Risk Monitor, Global Edition 2016.[13]

There is consensus however that since the financial crisis there has been the growing perception that the possibility of a tail risk event is more of a reality than it was previously—66% of investors say this is a growing concern.

Although institutional investors' main goal is to maximize their risk adjusted return, the potential damage caused by a tail risk event means 58% are willing to sacrifice return for protection in this regard. However, in the same breath, investors are aware that fear of tail risk events has led to risk aversion and 51% say this is excessive.

The greatest change in institutional investors' concern regarding the investment environment is around a potential global economic slowdown. This is expected to have more of an impact this year compared to last year. A much higher number of investors

12 "RiskMonitor Asia-Pacific Edition 2016," allianzgi.hk, Last Modified June 21, 2016, https://www.allianzgi.hk/en/downloads/others/al5agi-risk-monitor-2016-ap-version.
13 Ibid.

(38%) say this is a risk to investment performance this year. The figure compares to 12% last year.[14]

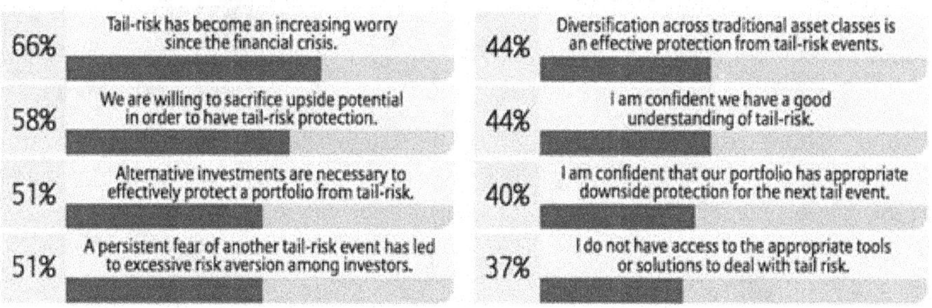

From Allianz Global Investors Risk Monitor, Global Edition 2016.[15]

The increased apprehension over the global economy is undoubtedly warranted. The last three months of 2015 recorded the slowest pace of global growth since 2012 when the European Union and Japan were both in recession. In the second week of April, the International Monetary Fund cut its outlook for 2016 economic growth for the fourth time in the past year, on the back of low oil prices, China's slowdown and chronic weakness in developed economies. Annualized global growth is now expected to be 3.2%, down from the 3.4 percent forecast in January.[16]

14 Ibid.
15 Ibid.
16 Ibid.

Risk to investment performance

The Americas	
Global economic slowdown	40%
Economic slowdown in China	32%
New banking crisis	30%

Europe and the Middle East	
Global economic slowdown	38%
New banking crisis	36%
Geopolitical tensions	35%

Asia Pacific	
Economic slowdown in China	45%
Geopolitical tensions	38%
Global economic slowdown	37%

Global	
Global economic slowdown	38%
Economic slowdown in China	37%
Geopolitical tensions	33%

From Allianz Global Investors Risk Monitor, Global Edition 2016.[17]

In a meeting in mid-April 2016, the International Monetary Fund Committee agreed that although global recovery is continuing, expansion is modest. Despite some improvement in the past months, the committee noted, "financial market volatility and risk aversion are rising amid questions about medium-term global growth prospects. The situation may ultimately weigh on sentiment..."

This is certainly being reflected in institutional investors' outlook.

A slowdown in China and a new banking crisis are the next two events where concern has risen sharply. This year, a greater number of think both of these will have a potentially negative impact on their investment performance.

After witnessing nearly three decades of double-digit growth, China has been showing signs of slowing down and has been replaced by India as the fastest growing major economy of the world. Concern regarding a new banking crisis is also justified to a certain extent. In February 2016, former Bank of England governor Mervyn King called for reform of the financial system, saying a crisis is "certain" otherwise.

The slowdown in China is more of a concern for investors in Asia-Pacific (45%) considering they feel more likely to be affected due

17 Ibid.

to geographical proximity. Interestingly a greater number of investors in this region feel geopolitical tensions will impact performance (38%). Fewer investors in the Americas echo this sentiment (27%).[18]

THE DIFFERENCE BETWEEN NORMAL RISK AND TAIL RISK

According to Investopedia, the definition of *tail risk* is "a form of portfolio risk that arises when the possibility that an investment will move more than three standard deviations from the mean is greater than what is shown by a normal distribution."[19] When a portfolio of investments is put together, it is assumed that the distribution of returns will follow a normal distribution. Under this assumption, the probability that returns will move between the mean and three standard deviations, either positively or negatively, is approximately 99.97 percent. The concept of tail risk suggests that the distribution is not normal but skewed and has fatter tails. The fatter tails increase the probability that an investment will move beyond three standard deviations.

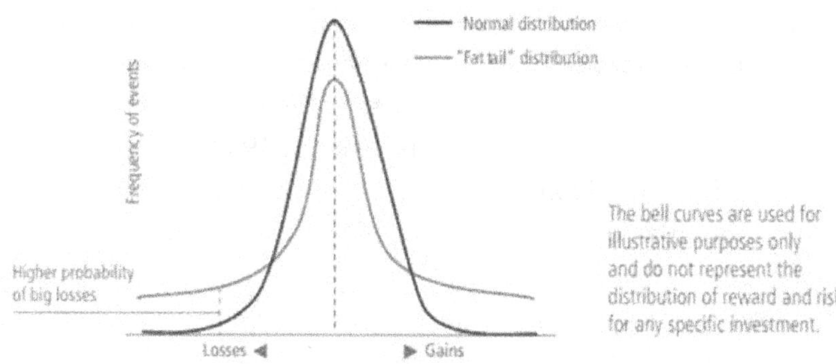

From the *Financial Times* lexicon.[20]

18 Ibid.

19 "Tail Risk Definition," Investopedia, accessed February 6, 2011, http://www.investopedia.com/terms/t/tailrisk.asp.

20 "Financial Times Lexicon Fat Tails," *Financial Times*, accessed May 4, 2017, http://lexicon.ft.com/Term?term=fat-tails.

In other words, tail risk is the risk of an asset or portfolio of assets moving more than three standard deviations from its current price. Most asset managers are only interested in the downside risk (i.e., moving more than three standard deviations below its current price; see Akoundi 2012; Bhansali 2008; Culp 2012; Karamjeet 2013, 2014, 2016; Newhouse 1982). The common technique of using a normal approximation to estimate the distribution of changes in price will underestimate the true value for tail risk due to fat tails in financial data. Tail risk is sometimes defined less strictly, as merely the risk (or probability) of rare events (Akoundi and Haugh 2012).

RATIONALE FOR TAIL RISK MANAGEMENT

The way conventional risk management is practiced does not seem to differentiate tail risk from "normal" risk. However, tail risk (low-probability, extreme-severity events; see Taleb 2010) has a very different nature, drivers, and magnitude of effects. Therefore, a separate approach for tail risk is required. The one-size-fits-all approach does not work here, and what the regulators have created looks very much like that.

The old-fashioned risk management framework was built to deal with normal risk (under a standard normal assumption) and often fails to provide an effective response when a tail risk event unfolds. That is because, unlike "normal" risk, tail risk often comes unmeasured and unpredicted and stems from unknown unknowns (Newhouse 1982).

Financial firms traditionally manage risk with a one-dimensional focus, even though a second dimension arising from extreme tail risk has very different implications (Karamjeet 2013). Traditional risk management, based on probability theory, works well for revenue models because when priced properly, compensation for quantifiable uncertainty can drive the revenue engine (Strischek 2014). In addition, the price of a mistake under conventional risk management may be only a fall in profits. However, the other dimension—extreme tail risk—needs to be handled differently, because the cost of being wrong can mean the difference between the life and death of the institution.

In other words, the lens of conventional risk management is first and foremost designed to manage and protect revenue opportunities (Karamjeet 2014b). Because of the limitations of a statistically based probability approach, this lens is incapable of objectively refracting an extreme tail risk exposure, which can be devastating for the firm.

From an uncertainty perspective, traditional risk management deals with specific outcomes that are unknown, but extrapolated expected loss values can be quantified and thus become known. And capital management deals with known scenarios, but their occurrences are unknown and cannot be quantified, and thus stress testing focuses on specific situations. However, tail risk management relates to unknown scenarios that cannot be envisioned, and thus their occurrences are also unknown (hence the need for reverse stress testing, scenario planning, risk mapping, and early warning).

Uncertainty management needs to focus beyond the pricing of risk, as actual results are also determined by how unknown events and market conditions can unfold. And, in extreme scenarios, unexpected losses can exceed the capital and thus threaten the survival of the institution. Therefore, tail risk management must leverage resources to mitigate and absorb unexpected losses in such a way that the capital (firm) is always protected and preserved.

The bottom line is tail risk management is about spelling out needed counteractions if there is a disruption of business activities regardless of the cause of the interruption, be it operational, financial, or geopolitical. Tail risk management must go beyond going-concern objectives; it's about survival. Now, granted, measures like living will, higher capital adequacy, and liquidity constraints do improve the survivability of the firm, but they do not prepare the firm in the event of extreme financial volatility.

Financial crises are a part of economic cycles; however, their impact on financial institutions and the financial system can be managed. An unequivocal focus on extreme tail risk will enhance the going-concern sustainability of institutions in a crisis and thus lead to a stronger financial system. A fundamental change is needed.

TAIL RISK CULTURE AND CONCEPTS

A distinct spectrum with its own objective parameters is needed for effective TRM to protect institutions from becoming casualties in crises. This can be done by turning to the following concepts (many of which, marked with an asterisk, find their applications in the nonbanking world):

- Risk mapping
- Early-warning systems
- Loss, threat, and vulnerability assessment*
- Supply chain risk management*
- Risk exposure index*
- Time to recover*
- Scenario planning
- Reverse stress testing
- Probable maximum loss*
- Financial continuity planning
- High-reliability organizations*
- Sustainable/resilient business model*

Risk managers need to change to an approach that emphasizes resiliency instead of the traditional threat-centric approach. The range of catastrophic events from 9/11 to the 2008 and 2010 financial crises to hurricanes, not to mention the arrival of cyber intrusions, has distinctively disabused risk managers of the notion that the purpose of risk management is to eliminate risk.

To be clear, risk is to be managed; it is not something that can entirely be avoided (Culp 2012). In the latter half of the twentieth century (mainly by the actions of the Basel committee and regulators alike), we naïvely believed that we could reduce risk to near zero. In the process, we started to lose some skill sets we need when a risk does manifest itself. However, while many sought to suppress risk at its source, this view has progressively given way to a more nuanced assessment that, because risk cannot entirely be sidestepped, a risk manager's chief determinations should necessitate erecting an enterprise stout enough to tolerate risks when they do occur.

Everyone will recognize that capital is the primary and ultimate driver of defense against unexpected losses from unquantifiable uncertainty. Thus, the goal in managing unquantifiable uncertainty is to preserve and shield capital from extreme risks.

However, risk management and TRM have such different objectives and inspirations that one cannot be merely extended to manage the other. Risk management drives a firm's revenue apparatus (Karamjeet 2014a), while TRM preserves the firm's survivability (but keep in mind that TRM is more than merely capital management).

Therefore, relying on risk management to manage just-in-case risks (or extreme financial risk) is a calamity waiting to happen, as shown by the events of 2008 and 2010. Indeed, despite the sophistication, advancement, and investment of massive resources in risk management during the 1990s and early 2000s, a disaster did happen: the GFC.

Every year, around $100 billion is globally invested in governance, risk, and compliance resources, and the market is only expected to grow, reaching $120 billion in the next five years (Lundstrom 2014). Financial institution spending on compliance has also increased as a percentage of total expenditure.

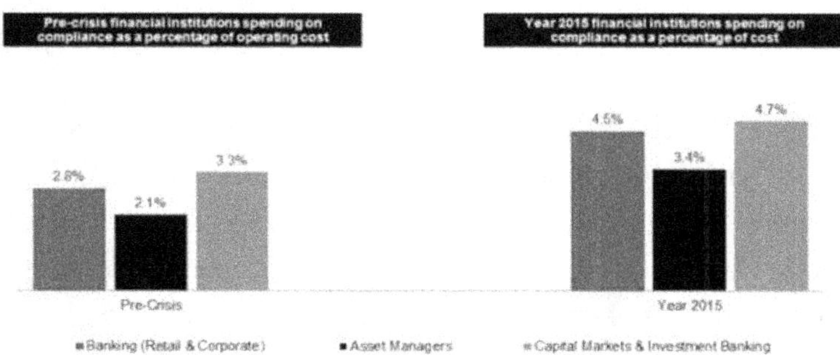

From Amit Goel, "How Can RegTechs Help Financial Services Industry Overcome the Burden of Compliance?"[21]

21 A. Goel, "How Can RegTechs Help Financial Services Industry Overcome the Burden of Compliance?," Let's Talk Payments, Last Modified May 9, 2016, https://letstalkpayments.com/how-can-regtechs-help-financial-services-industry-overcome-the-burden-of-compliance/.

We are taught that efficiency and maximizing shareholder value do not tolerate redundancy. Indeed, most executives do not realize that optimization and lean structures make companies vulnerable to changes in the environment. Biological systems cope with change; Mother Nature is the best risk manager of all (Taleb,2009). That is partly because she loves redundancy. Evolution has given us spare parts—we have two lungs and two kidneys, for instance—that allow us to survive.

Indeed, redundancy is rarely unambiguously unspoiled or managed, but is just as important as the mixture in providing resilience (Boin 2010). Focus should be centered on important functions or services with low redundancy, such as those controlled by key species or actors. In some cases, it may be possible to increase the redundancy coupled with these functions.

In the corporate world, redundancy comprises outward inefficiency: idle capacities, unused parts, and money not put to work. The reverse is leverage, which we are taught is good. However, it is not; debt makes businesses—and the economic system that goes with it—brittle (Taleb 2012).

If a business is highly leveraged, it could go under if the company neglects a sales forecast, interest rates change, or other risks that occur. If a business is not carrying debt on the books, it can cope better with changes.

Unfortunately, existing regulatory developments (such as Basel III, EMIR, and Dodd-Frank) are not real incentives for safeguards against extreme financial events. Meeting regulatory requirements does not equal managing extreme tail risk adequately, and senior leadership, for the sake of preserving the interests of the various stakeholders, should think beyond what is legally required from them.

In summary, TRM is about illustrating the needed counteractions if there is a disruption of business activities, regardless of the cause of the interruption, be it operational, financial, or geopolitical. TRM must go beyond the optimization of profits; it is about survival. Measures like the living will, higher capital adequacy, lower leverage, and liquidity constraints do improve the survivability of the firm, but they do not prepare the firm enough in the event of extreme financial volatility.

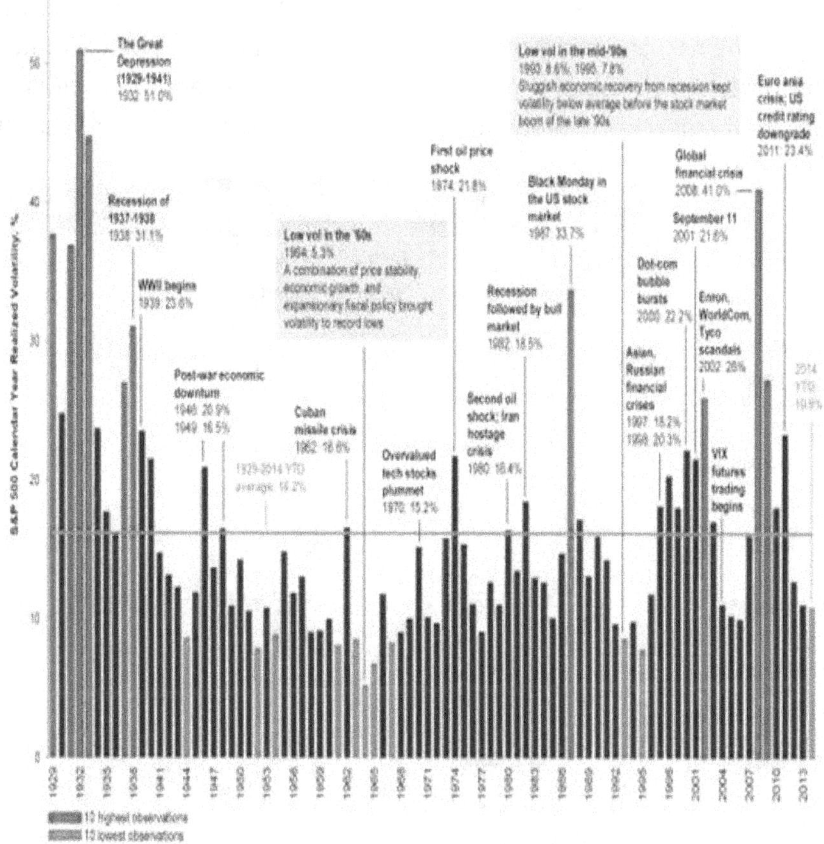

From T. Durden, "The Annotated History of Global Volatility," *ZeroHedge*, June 26, 2014.

As the above graph illustrates, regardless of perspective, financial crises are just a part of economic cycles. However, their effect on financial institutions and the financial system can be managed.

HOW BASEL III MISSED THE POINT

Over the past years, whether in the United States, Australia, or Western Europe, there was news that regulators planned to require large financial institutions to have a higher level of capital in the form of a surcharge amount of capital. These new requirements are deemed to be "aimed at reducing the risk, and the required increase in capital would be calibrated to the relative riskiness of the firm as measured by a series of factors."[22] These are the new capital requirements (in comparison to the old Basel II):

	Basel II			Basel III		
	Common Equity	Tier 1 Capital	Tier 2 Capital	Common Equity	Tier 1 Capital	Tier 2 Capital
Minimum Requirements	2%	4%	8%	4.5%	6%	8%
Capital Conservation Buffer		Not applicable		2.5%		
Countercyclical Capital Buffer		Not applicable		0% to 2.5%		
Leverage Ratio		Not applicable			Tier 1 Leverage Ratio ≥ 3% *	
Liquidity Coverage Ratio		Not applicable			≥ 100%	
Net Stable Funding Ratio		Not applicable			≥ 100%	

From EY Global Regulatory Network.[23]

Notwithstanding the good intentions of the Basel Committee, while higher capital requirements will certainly prevent financial institutions

22 V. McGrane and R. Tracy, "Fed to Hit Bog Banks with Stiffer Surcharge," *Wall Street Journal*, September 9, 2014.

23 D. Martin, "Basel III Challenges, Impact and Consequences, March 2012," EY Global Regulatory Network, accessed April 2, 2017, https://www.eycom.ch/en/Publications/20120323-Basel-3-challenges-impact-and-consequences/download.

from engaging in too risky activities, it will not shield them from future unexpected events.

And that's where Basel III provides a false sense of security—there is no such thing as safety in numbers. Safety goes beyond numbers—it's a question of building a resilient business model.

Therefore, there is no rapport between expected losses from normal risk and the maximum potential losses from tail risk, as these are two self-governing factors. Both must be managed concurrently and plainly, as they affect firms very differently.

The price of a mistake in relation to normal risk is the loss of profits; the price of a mistake with extreme tail risk can be mortal to organizations. Treating severe risk as an annex of normal risk and relying merely on more robust capital requirements is a calamity waiting to happen.

Recall that what triggered the failures in 2008 was not "too much risk," but rather "too much (extreme) tail risk"—a key distinction. While recent actions have targeted "too much risk," none has fully addressed the "extreme risk" vulnerability. Today there are not even metrics to quantify it, without which one cannot demonstrably tackle how much severe risk is too much or how much capital is needed to protect against it.

Financial firm failures in a crisis always come as a surprise because, without a measure, even management does not know how close to the edge of the extreme risk precipice their institution is, and thus senior executives remain unaware of their firm's vulnerability (e.g., London Whale at JPMorgan Chase Bank in a different setting).

Capital guidelines based on objective and transparent metrics of extreme risk would fundamentally address the risk to ensure financial institutions' sustainability in crises and thus strengthen the financial system. Anything less leaves the problem unaddressed, with the real culprit lurking around unwittingly at best and compounding risks over time at worst.

But unfortunately, such quantitative guidelines to tackle unexpected events do not yet exist. In the meantime, in the absence of such extreme risk metrics, we shall do well with qualitative risk metrics.

Financial crises are just part of economic cycles and will happen again. The only sure way to survive them is to grasp extreme risk now and manage it proactively. Financial firms have precise metrics for profits and volatility from normal risk. Should there not be one for extreme risk that causes devastation in financial crises? As already mentioned, the answer is simply no.

A better way to manage these extreme risks in the case of a black swan event is to develop and build a more resilient business model that focuses on reinforced business and control processes combined with a strong risk awareness culture.

HOW BASEL III PUT IN PLACE INHERENT PROCYCLICAL MEASURES AND TOOLS

One of the key elements of Basel III is putting in place a countercyclical buffer. The countercyclical buffer has been introduced in order to increase capital requirements in good times and decrease the same in bad times. The buffer will slow banking activity when it overheats and will encourage lending when times are tough. The buffer will range from 0 to 2.5 percent, consisting of common equity or other fully loss-absorbing capital.

Still, notwithstanding this countercyclical objective, Basel III is wrong about mitigating procyclicality in the sense that, firstly, regulatory risk weights change countercyclicality—that is, risk weights increase during economic downturns and decrease during upturns. This shows that countercyclical regulatory risk weights only serve to further exacerbate any accounting leverage procyclicality. And secondly, the Basel III higher capital buffers will amplify even more business cycle fluctuations, forcing banks to restrict their lending even further when the economy goes into recession.

The following table from BIS mirrors how the risk weights are changing relative to credit ratings, namely, the lower the credit rating, the higher the risk weights, and hence the higher the risk-weighted assets.

Table 1: Risk-weights for credit risk in Basel II (standardised approach) and in Basel I

Portfolio			Basel II (standardised approach) AAA to AA-	A+ to A-	BBB+ to BBB-	BB+ to BB-	B+ to B-	Below B-	Not rated	Basel I OECD	Non-OECD
Corporate			20%	50%	100%	100%	150%	150%	100%	100%	100%
Bank *	Option 1		20%	50%	100%	100%	100%	150%	100%		
	Option 2	LT	20%	50%	50%	100%	100%	150%	50%	LT 20%	100%
		ST	20%	20%	20%	50%	50%	150%	20%	ST 20%	20%
Sovereign			0%	20%	50%	100%	100%	150%	100%	0%	100%

Note: * The distinction between Option 1 (risk-weight one category below that of the sovereign) and Option 2 (risk-weight based on the rating of the bank) applies only in Basel II

Source: Basel Committee on Banking Supervision (2004)

Additionally, during periods of economic boom, financial institutions tend to have their lending portfolios increasing, while when there is an economic downturn, those same financial institutions will try to curtail their lending activities.

In reality, banks anticipate the cyclical position of the economy and may hold capital in excess of the regulatory requirements. Poorly capitalized banks that face materializing credit risk in a bust have two options in order to avoid falling below the minimum capital requirement. They can either raise capital, or they can increase their capital buffers through a reduction of risk-weighted assets. Both options have drawbacks. Consequently, a decrease in risk-weighted assets can be attained through a decrease in lending. If this reduction in lending is stronger than the decrease in loan demand, then the recession is further amplified.

STAKEHOLDERS IN TAIL RISK MANAGEMENT

Merely complying with regulatory requirements does not equate to managing extreme tail risk adequately. Senior leadership, for the sake of preserving the interests of the various stakeholders (clients, regulators, taxpayers, government, employees, shareholders, lenders, etc.), should think beyond what is legally required from them.

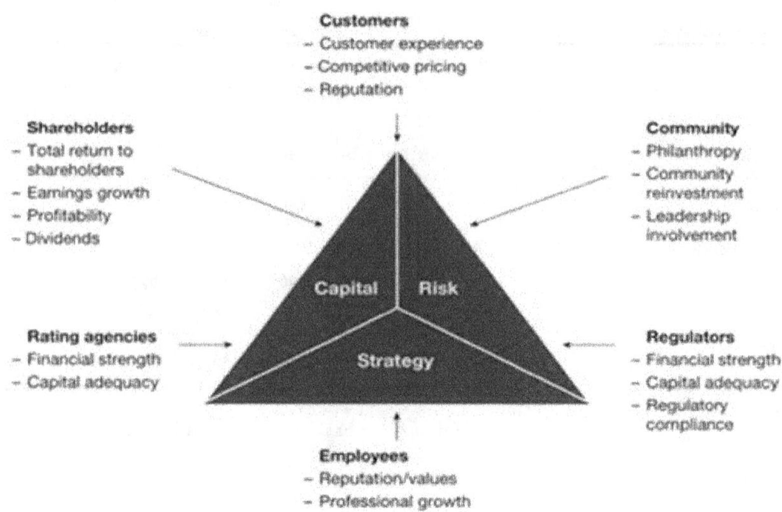

From Strategy Analysis.[24]

Basel III, the Dodd-Frank Act, and other domestic postcrisis regulations are not going away, and regulation will remain a major constraint on financial firms and will keep the cost of capital high and the return on equity challenging.

To adjust to the postcrisis financial environment, financial firms must adapt their capital management and capital planning programs not only to comply with regulations but also to improve the efficiency of their use of capital with the aim of building a more resilient business model.[25]

---

24 Booz & Co, "A Comprehensive Risk Appetite Framework for Banks," PWC, accessed May 4, 2017, https://www.strategyand.pwc.com/media/file/Risk_Appetite_Framework.pdf.

25 A. Meyer, "Planning for Profitability," London: *Banking Technology*. September 14, 2014, http://www.bankingtech.com/60651/planning-for-profitability/

Tail Risk Management Is Not an Extension of Day-to-Day Risk Management

WHAT TAIL RISK MANAGEMENT IS NOT

One way of understanding tail risk management is to think about what tail risk management is not. Let's take five minutes to compare and contrast tail risk management and other related concepts.

Tail risk management is not about constantly worrying. It's not about fretting and constructing worst-case scenarios. A tail risk management program is not designed to freeze an organization because of the fear of what might happen.

It is instead about exercising informed judgment to manage our environments, to assess what realistically might happen, to control what we can control, to take advantage of opportunities that are worth pursuing, and to achieve our goals.

Tail risk management is not about strategic planning. No doubt, you and your organizations have gone through strategic planning processes in which you have done a SWOT analysis, which looks at strengths, weaknesses, opportunities, and threats. Yes, we do talk about threats and opportunities in tail risk management, and we focus on building our strengths and reducing weaknesses.

But the emphasis in a tail risk management program is dynamic. Furthermore, where strategic planning projects into the future what an organization would like to do, tail risk management focuses on identifying the weakest links and how to avoid the slipups that could undermine the existence of the firm.

Tail risk management is not about the adequacy of (economic) capital. Studies show that meeting regulatory capital requirements is no assurance of survival in a crisis. Per "federal law and OTS regulations...an institution is treated as well-capitalized when...its Tier 1 risk-based capital ratio is 6.00% or greater," said the 2007 annual report of Washington Mutual, which appeared to be in fine fettle with a Tier I ratio of 6.84 percent before its collapse.

The need for a larger cushion is real, but it must objectively relate to the extreme tail risk that creates this need. Simply requiring higher capital is no assurance that a fundamental problem has been addressed.

Tail risk management is not about hedging. Rather, it is more about solid portfolio risk management skills that also embody just-in-case risk management. Tail risk management is much more than shielding asset returns from unexpected events.

Tail risk management is about protecting the firm or fund's capital from sudden massive losses as well as about sustainability.

Tail risk management is not about avoiding risks. Risk is to be managed; it cannot entirely be avoided. Up until the early twenty-first century, we thought that through financial modeling and probability theories we could reduce risk to near zero. However, the recent GFC in 2008 took a hard toll on many financial firms, as they had lost in the process some skill sets to address emerging risks when they manifest themselves. Those skill sets need to be regained, and tail risk management can be a useful approach to reach that objective.

Tail risk management is not about enterprise risk management. As a risk manager, it is not enough that I have used enterprise risk management to identify, prioritize, treat, and monitor risks. I am also required to consider the black swans after this process and analyze whether more needs to be done. "The natural tendency to become complacent—'I have done enough thinking'—is countered by asking,

'Have I done enough thinking?' and 'Am I ignoring residual risk?'"[26] At the end of the day, it's a matter of behaving professionally at all times and being keen to create an added value that will protect and even help grow the business.

Tail risk management is not about auditing. "Auditing is usually performed by accountants, and it usually is performed in order to determine whether financial statements are presented in accordance with generally accepted accounting principles."[27]

Tail risk management may draw on auditing procedures. For instance, risk management might involve sampling, verification of data, tracing information, and reporting results. But getting an audit—and receiving a "clean" or unqualified audit opinion—is not the same as having a tail risk management program. The two are very different.

An organization with no tail risk management program may get a clean audit opinion by presenting its financial information in conformity with GAAP, and an organization with a tail "risk management program may receive an adverse audit opinion (by having material misstatements that undermine the accuracy of the organization's financial reports)."[28]

Tail risk management is not about financial models. Financial institutions openly opt to continue to rely on traditional risk management fed by probabilities tailored by financial models as well as by big data (under the auspices of the banking regulators, one must say), not to mention the traditional risk control methods to track down tail risk events.

But whichever way you look at it, tail events occur much more frequently than Gaussian distributions and data mining imply, and concentrations are not always sufficient to identify pockets of tail risks.

---

26 D. Zavatsky, "Complacency: The Greatest Risk of All," *Food Safety News*, February 19, 2013, http://www.foodsafetynews.com/2013/02/complacency-the-greatest-risk-of-all/.

27 T. Bilich, "What Risk Management Is Not," Risk Alternatives, http://risk-alternatives.com/what-risk-management-is-not/.

28 Ibid.

Given increased global capital mobility since the early 1980s, the frequency, magnitude, and complexity of financial crises appear to be increasing, and no financial model will ever be able to grasp that fully.

Finally, tail risk management is not the entirety of management. Management, generally speaking, includes supervision, motivation, discipline, and a host of other activities that coordinate efforts within an organization. Tail risk management is a part of overall management, but it is not all of it.

THREE LINES OF DEFENSE

In the "three lines of defense" model, business lines are the first lines of defense in risk management, as they own the risk, while the various control and compliance oversight functions resting with the risk management function act as the second line of defense, and independent assurance is the third line of defense.

Within the financial services sector, risk management traditionally takes the form of erection of external defenses through global and national regulations. Internal defenses habitually take the form of the three lines of defense model, which portrays three parties as the core to good risk management:

1. Operational staff within the business who take frontline responsibility for assessing, measuring, and monitoring risks
2. Risk management function
3. Internal auditing whose role is to provide board-level assurance on the effectiveness of internal controls

However, there are several problems. This model is not what usually happens, and it would not be desirable if it did:

- √ First, managers in these control functions seldom collaborate with operations managers. Control processes are usually developed in isolation from operating managers and other control functions. Collaboration is rare and coordination more so.

- √ Second, control processes do not constitute a line of defense in most circumstances. Most controls are detective rather than preventive. Only preventive controls constitute a line of defense and then only at the operating level (therefore, they are an essential element of the "first line of defense"), which is where the metaphor breaks down. Detective controls allow intervention and workarounds to address a problem after the fact. That is not a line of defense; it is a line of remediation.
- √ Third, the role of the internal audit is also not a line of defense. It is, or should be, the provision of comfort that operating functions are properly specified from a control perspective; that preventive controls, where feasible, are developed and operating effectively; and that, where they are not, detective or compensating controls are instituted and monitored and remedial action is subsequently taken.
- √ Lastly, to think of an internal audit as a line of defense is asinine. It does not and should not do any such thing. It is not operating either preventively or "detectively" at a transactional level. It is there to provide assurance that operating management is fulfilling its control job and that support managers are supporting operating managers to do so. It is not there to intervene in the normal transaction flow as a control stage.

That is why in Australia and New Zealand, for example, internal auditing is not part of the third line of defense; instead, there is a dedicated department called assurance that embodies the third line of defense. While the "three lines of defense" model for risk management has been accepted as a best practice by banking regulators and the Basel Committee on Banking Supervision, the internal audit function should be replaced by a risk assurance function.

The assurance department's responsibilities include the following, among others:

- Assisting in the development of the overall strategy and approach to risk and compliance assurance in line with the risk management framework, anti–money laundering (AML), and compliance management framework
- Developing the AML and compliance assurance plan and ensuring this takes a risk-based approach in identifying areas to be assessed and monitored throughout the year
- Collaborating with managers and peers to ensure that the AML and compliance assurance plan is coordinated with other risk assurance classes to minimize gaps and overlaps and to provide end-to-end coverage across organizational boundaries
- Reviewing and revising plans to reflect changes in the risk and compliance environment
- Ensuring delivery of AML and compliance assurance in accordance with the plan
- Reporting to management on findings of substance and working with them to resolve issues and improve operational risk management in their area
- Tracking the resolution of significant issues identified during assurance activity
- Providing concise, integrated risk reporting on the effectiveness of AML and compliance risk management
- Assisting to develop and maintain strong relationships with external and internal auditors to achieve a coordinated and integrated program of assurance for the division

THE THREE LINES OF DEFENSE MODEL COULD BE A SWISS CHEESE

The Swiss cheese model portrays risk management as a series of slices of cheese that act as defenses against the impact of "holes" or ineffective controls that may arise because of either active failures in control systems (e.g., IT breakdown) or latent conditions that can cause holes in the defense slices. These latter conditions are caused by inherent weaknesses in the defenses that increase their susceptibility to failure, such as an organizational culture that does not see risk management as important.

In other words:

> Defenses, barriers, and safeguards occupy a key position in the system approach. High technology systems have many defensive layers: some are engineered (alarms, physical barriers, automatic shutdowns, etc), others rely on people (surgeons, anesthetists, pilots, control room operators, etc), and yet others depend on procedures and administrative controls. Their function is to protect potential victims and assets from local hazards. Mostly they do this very effectively, but there are always weaknesses.
>
> In an ideal world each defensive layer would be intact. In reality, however, they are more like slices of Swiss cheese, having many holes—though unlike in the cheese, these holes are continually opening, shutting, and shifting their location. The presence of holes in any one "slice" does not normally cause a bad outcome. Usually, this can happen only when the holes in many layers momentarily line up to permit a trajectory of accident opportunity—bringing hazards into damaging contact with victims.[29]
>
> The holes in the defenses arise for two reasons: active failures and latent conditions. Nearly all adverse events involve a combination of these two sets of factors. Active failures are the unsafe acts committed by people who are in direct contact with the patient or system. They take a variety of forms: slips, lapses, fumbles, mistakes, and procedural violations. Active failures have a direct and usually shortlived impact on the integrity of the defenses.[30]

29
30

A recent illustrative example of an active failure is the infamous incident that took place in Fukushima, Japan, in March 2011 when operators (TEPCO) did a poor risk assessment and collateral damage management, leading to a domino effect with the tragic consequences we all know. Followers of the person approach often look no further for the causes of an adverse event once they have identified these proximal unsafe acts. But virtually all such acts have a causal history that extends back in time and up through the levels of the system. Indeed, latent conditions arise from decisions made by not only designers and builders but also top-level management. Such decisions may be mistaken, but they need not be. All such strategic decisions have the potential for introducing viruses into the system.

Latent conditions—as the term suggests—may be a sleeping disease that lurks beneath the surface within the system for many years before combining with active failures and local triggers to create an accident opportunity. The good news is that latent conditions can be identified and remedied before an adverse event occurs; understanding this leads to proactive rather than reactive risk management.

With respect to active failures, while we cannot alter the human condition, we can change the conditions under which humans work. To use another analogy: active failures are like rodents. They can be killed one by one, but they still keep coming. The best remedies are to create more effective defenses and to clean up the sewers in which they breed. The sewers, in this case, are the ever-present latent conditions.

The risk imbalances may occur within a company's control environment, risk architecture, or the overall information and understanding of risk. If the imbalances are redefined, then one-off holes may not matter. A company can manage isolated failures in its control system.

If, however, many different holes occur together and are aligned, then the overall system comes under threat of failure, even if the individual lines of defense are in place. That is the risk with the Swiss cheese model. Citibank, Barclays, RBS, Fortis, UBS, and so on provide examples of how seemingly good defense systems can be undermined by risk imbalances.

The powerful latent forces of a segmented business model, combined with a lack of common purpose about risk management across the firm, ultimately produce the ingredients for failure. There is an element of hazard in the fact that the holes may or may not align, but if they do align, then problems abound. The central lesson of the Swiss cheese model is that defense structures alone are not sufficient. How they interact is also of critical importance, but this is a matter of human relations and issues of relative knowledge and power.[31]

ENTERPRISE RISK MANAGEMENT AND TAIL RISK MANAGEMENT

Prior to discussing the interaction between ERM and TRM, let's quickly look at how ERM differs from traditional risk management.

Among the most significant issues inhibiting effective and efficient risk management is what we call the "silo factor." Typically, risk is assigned to risk managers within departments: the finance department monitors credit risk, public relations oversees reputation risk, facilities management supervises physical risk, IT focuses on data security risk, and so on. Now, while this level of specialization is essential, compartmentalizing risk managers in these silos results in a narrow, parochial view of risk and prevents top management from understanding risks facing the entire enterprise.

Therefore, looking at risk across business segments and from both the bottom-up and top-to-bottom perspectives can really help companies see what risks they need to monitor most. As such, ERM has become the alpha and omega in most advanced organizations, whether in the financial or nonfinancial sector.

In other words, ERM distinguishes itself from traditional risk management in several aspects, the most significant of which is that it considers risks from the enterprise perspective as opposed to risks that originate and are managed within functional silos or specific business units of an organization.

31 Ibid.

So, in practice, this means that the ERM function will have an overall helicopter view on all the risks that affect the financial firm (credit risk, market risk, liquidity risk, funding risk, operational risk, interest rate risk, legal risk, IT risk, reputation risk, etc.) and will integrate the findings of each risk area with concepts on internal controls and strategic planning. Given its scope, ERM is deemed capable of addressing the needs of various stakeholders who want to understand the broad spectrum of risks facing complex organizations to ensure they are appropriately managed.

Typically, this involves identifying particular events or circumstances relevant to the organization's objectives (risks and opportunities), assessing them in terms of likelihood and magnitude of impact, determining a response strategy, and monitoring progress.

Unfortunately, many of these organizations that do embrace an ERM framework tend to continue to focus mainly on near-term (predictable and quantifiable) risks without paying adequate attention to "emerging risks" (i.e., those risk issues that have not manifested themselves sufficiently to be managed using the tools commonly applied to more developed exposures and with those that have a low likelihood).

Hence, there is a "cry in the dark" for allowing ERM to evolve in the near future into emerging risk management rather than traditional enterprise risk management. Emerging risks are those risks an organization has not yet recognized or those that are known to exist but are not well understood (Diebold 2010). These are Donald Rumsfeld's famous "known unknowns" and "unknown unknowns."

Nowadays, an ERM program that does not address the potential challenges created by the existence and development of emerging risks will not meet its goal of protecting and generating opportunity for the organization. Indeed, the recent GFC, which was identified early by some risk managers as an emerging risk, raised many serious questions, some of which focused on the effectiveness of risk management practices and, more specifically, ERM.

There was a failure to use enterprise risk management to inform management's decision making for both risk-taking and risk-avoiding decisions. There was also a failure to embed the best practices of ERM from the top all the way down to the trading floor, with the mistaken assumption that there is only one way to view a particular risk.

Senior leadership may sponsor the development of an ERM program, but that is not enough for its foundational principles to take root and flourish. Behavior at the highest levels of the organization, at the parent and subsidiary level reinforced through risk-performance measurement, builds a culture of risk-adjusted decision making throughout an organization. The techniques and methodology must be used comprehensively at every level of the enterprise.

But more than that, ERM failed to foresee the GFC and will continue to do so unless a cultural change takes place that embraces the concept of TRM. Even more so, executives must endorse and support the successful implementation of TRM.

OPERATIONAL RISK MANAGEMENT AND TAIL RISK MANAGEMENT

The risk management of disruptive events is partially covered by operational risk management. Indeed, operational risk can be created by a wide range of different external events, ranging from power failures to floods or earthquakes to terrorist attacks.

Similarly, operational risk can arise due to internal events, such as the potential for failures or inadequacies in any of the bank's processes and systems (e.g., IT, risk management, or human resource management processes and systems), or those of its outsourced service providers.

Under a typical operational risk management (ORM) framework, the financial firm assesses the potential risk for such events to happen and designs and implements disaster recovery systems and procedures with a view to ensuring continuity of activity (also known as the business recovery plan). Additionally, against the monetary loss derived from such operational events, the firm evaluates the potential cost and puts in place proper mitigation techniques.

As already mentioned, operational risk can equally arise from human resource mismanagement, such as mismanaged or poorly trained employees, employee negligence or willful misconduct, conflicts of interest, fraud, and rogue trading. Therefore, the emergence of mistrust, failure to communicate, low morale, increased turnover, and cynicism among staff members are regarded as early-warning signs for a potential increase in operational risk.

However, geofinancial trigger events are not covered by operational risk management, such as a market crash, the spillover effects of the bankruptcy of a systemically important financial institution, the effect of a Grexit/Brexit/Frexit, a very hard landing of the Chinese economy, a military confrontation between the West and Russia in Central Europe, the takeover of Saudi Arabia by ISIS, and the escalating conflict between China and the Philippines. All these geofinancial events will, in one way or another from a supply chain management perspective, disrupt the provisions of financial services by the firm to the end customer.

And that's where tail risk management comes into play by also taking into account nonoperational events that might affect the existence of the firm's business model.

LIMITATIONS OF ERM AND ORM

While processes such as ERM and ORM can help companies avoid financial market and supply chain disruptions, as well as recover normal operations quickly, they also have serious limitations[32]:

- First, they rely too heavily on risk identification. In a complex and turbulent global supply network, many of the risks that a company faces are unpredictable or unknowable before the event happens. These "emergent" risks are often triggered by improbable events whose causes are not understood, and their potential cascading effects are difficult to understand a priori. Clearly, it would be impractical for companies to identify and

32 J. Fiksel, "From Risk to Resilience: Learning to Deal with Disruption," MIT Sloan Management Review & Report, 2015, http://tribunecontentagency.com/article/from-risk-to-resilience-learning-to-deal.

investigate all the potential risks that may be hidden in their global supply chains.

- Second, ERM and ORM depend on statistical information that may not exist. Risk assessments are limited by the quality and credibility of the assumptions on which they are based, and faulty assumptions or data can lead to misallocation of resources. Of particular challenge are low-probability, high-consequence events for which there is little empirical knowledge; managers may underestimate the probabilities of these events or the magnitudes of their consequences because they have never experienced them.
- Third, the traditional ERM process of risk identification, assessment, mitigation, and monitoring is based on a simplified, "reductionist" view of the world. Each risk is identified and addressed independently, and hidden interactions are seldom recognized. This procedural approach can lull organizations into a false sense of complacency that could be shattered by an unexpected event (for instance, an oil spill in the Gulf of Mexico).

The complex, dynamic nature of global financial markets and supply chains requires constant vigilance to discern systemic vulnerabilities, as well as exceptional agility and flexibility when disruptions occur.

Organizations need to improve how they deal with financial market and supply chain complexity and unexpected disruptions so that they can prosper in the face of turbulent change. Organizations tend to become less resilient as they grow more complex. However, they can cultivate resilience by understanding their vulnerabilities and developing specific capabilities to cope with disruptions.

They can try to emulate some of the behaviors seen in natural systems—tolerance for variability, continuous adaptation, and exploitation of opportunities created by disruptive forces. Depending on the type of disturbance, the adaptation can be rapid or gradual.

RESILIENCY MANAGEMENT AND JUST-IN-CASE RISK MANAGEMENT

Resilient systems don't fail in the face of disturbances; rather, they adapt. But at the end of the day, the best risk method to manage emerging risks, even those that you cannot define or quantify, is to implement a tail risk management framework. The idea is not to prevent tail risks from occurring, but rather to build a resiliency in the business model to face and mitigate the effects of a black swan event. Tail risk management helps senior executives in looking at emerging risks as positive disruptors, and not as threats sabotaging the mere existence of the company. As such, tail risk management embraces disruption—through tail risk management, the company builds a business model that welcomes uncertainty and volatility.

Generally speaking, firms have an implicit objective to protect their going concerns. However, there are very few, if any, explicit, objective, and transparent links between a sustainability or resiliency objective and an institution's operations. Everyday operations are run to capture the full potential of a firm's business model within stated policies and limits, without an explicit link to the implicit resiliency objective. The net result is that institutions end up managing extreme tail risk through implicit and subjective mechanisms.

As mentioned earlier, simplistically relying on traditional risk management to manage just-in-case risks (or extreme financial risk) is a catastrophe waiting to happen, as shown by the recent events of 2008. Indeed, despite the sophistication, advancement, and investment of resources in risk management during the last decade, a disaster did happen—the GFC.

From an uncertainty perspective, traditional risk management deals with specific outcomes that are unknown, but extrapolated expected loss values can be quantified and thus become known. Furthermore, capital management deals with known scenarios, but their occurrences are unknown and cannot be quantified, and thus stress testing focuses on specific situations. However, TRM relates to unknown scenarios that cannot be envisioned; thus, their occurrences are also unknown (hence, the need for reverse stress testing, scenario planning, risk mapping, and early warning).

TAIL EVENTS AND PORTFOLIO RISK MANAGEMENT

In the world of financial markets, tail risk is defined as

> a form of portfolio risk that arises when the possibility that an investment will move more than three standard deviations from the mean is greater than what is shown by a normal distribution. Tail risks include events that have a small probability of occurring and occur at the ends of a normal distribution curve.
>
> Traditional portfolio strategies typically follow the idea that market returns follow a normal distribution. However, the concept of tail risk suggests that the distribution of returns is not normal, but skewed, and has fatter tails. The fat tails indicate that there is a probability, which may be small, that an investment will move beyond three standard deviations. Distributions that are characterized by fat tails are often seen when looking at hedge fund returns.[33]

Indeed, several quantitative methods exist with the aim to reduce tail risk in an investment portfolio. "One method is to limit asset allocation risk by weighting portfolios to less volatile sectors. Another method is keeping asset allocation constant, then complementing it with strategies such as equity puts, credit protection, currency and interest rate options."[34] And there are the strategies involving derivatives, but these require really special skills.

However, the downfall to these tail risk hedging strategies is that diversification does not work in the event of a systemic crisis. Not only is correlation analysis in credit portfolio management design overrated, but also correlation does not imply causation. As such, correlation in a stressed market environment does not make sense either, as deemed uncorrelated assets tend to converge to 1 in the event of a systemic crisis.

---

33 "Tail Risk Definition," Investopedia, http://www.investopedia.com/terms/t/tailrisk.asp.

34 M. Connor, "Education Series Understanding Tail Risk," Pimco, July 2014, https://www.pimco.com/en-us/resources/education/understanding-tail-risk/.

Last but not least, economic globalization has reduced the independence of international asset returns.

These phenomena diminish the diversification effect, which is the reduction in credit portfolio risk attributable to imperfect correlations between the returns of different portfolio assets. It is therefore important that credit portfolio risk managers focus clearly on the distinction between correlation and causation and not fall into the trap of assuming that the former implies the latter. As it relates to the use of derivatives, despite their growing demand, fewer and fewer market participants are willing or able to sell these products. Whereas an option buyer's risk is limited to the premium they pay, an option seller has much greater risk. Additionally, with the increase in the price of volatility, the cost of portfolio protection has also increased. "For investors trying to reach a certain return target, this high cost can be a constant drag on returns, preventing them from meeting return expectations."[35]

Therefore, from my perspective, TRM should go beyond merely tail risk hedging; it is more about solid portfolio risk management skills that need to embody just-in-case risk management. In other words, a robust TRM should be much more than shielding asset returns from unexpected events.

As already mentioned, TRM is about sustainability and protecting the firm or fund's capital from sudden massive losses. Not only do funds and firms alike need adequate capital and liquidity levels, but also they need to be built around a business line that is the comfort zone of both management and clients (in the case of client funds).

While TRM will not help the firm or fund predict the next extreme event, it will help shield the firm or fund's capital from the effects of an extreme event. TRM is much more than merely hedging—it is a state of mind supported by solid risk governance and IT resources ultimately aimed at sustaining the firm or fund's business model.

---

35 A. Gerstein, "The Challenges in Hedging Tail Risk," *New York Times*, April 20, 2012, https://dealbook.nytimes.com/2012/04/20/the-challenges-in-hedging-tail-risk/.

TAIL RISK MANAGEMENT: UNIQUE OPPORTUNITY ADDRESSING WEAKNESSES IN RISK MANAGEMENT

I believe that the current circumstances of increased volatility and uncertainty present a unique opportunity for financial firms to engage in such a tail risk management journey, transform their business model through a more robust risk management organization, and ultimately break free from the "overshoot-undershoot" swing pattern that often follows crises.

Financial companies that go the distance in this journey will position their organization to master the next series of challenges and gain a new competitive edge that allows them to take full advantage of future growth opportunities.

And in order to learn from the past, the top ten risk management mistakes that kill shareholder value, and for which TRM could provide an answer, are the following:

1. Studying the past as a guide to managing present and future risks
2. Managing risk by predicting extreme events
3. Maintaining the status quo
4. Not engaging enough with business partners
5. Compartmentalizing the different risk areas
6. Intertwining capital management with TRM
7. Assuming that mathematical models can replace solid underwriting
8. Being satisfied with merely complying with regulatory objectives
9. Managing a portfolio of risk exposures as a hold-to-maturity
10. Ignoring and mismanaging legal and contract risk

Interaction between Geopolitics and Financial Markets

INTRODUCTION OF THE CONCEPT OF GEOFINANCE

I am not the first to have used the term *geofinance*. Charles Goldfinger used the term in his book *La Geofinance—Pour Comprendre la Mutation Financière (Geofinance – Understanding Financial Transformation)* (1986). Geopolitical hotbeds from the Ukraine through the Middle East to the South China Sea are connected to economic and financial market pressures. Therefore, geopolitics as a tail event is not random and should not be considered an unknown unknowable (as most tail events are). Geopolitical events are part of the continuation of globalization and the integration trend in the global economy; thus, they can be anticipated with further analysis.

However, unfortunately, risk analysts and investors alike are largely unable to analyze the connection between these two points, as evidenced by how financial markets typically fail to respond to geopolitical developments until they culminate in graphic headlines (Copeland 2015). Given the current threat of geopolitical risk, it is reasonable to question why global financial markets remain so buoyant. How are geopolitics and financial markets interconnected? The reality is that geopolitical risk rarely poses a significant persistent threat to the broad financial markets until a full-blown crisis erupts. The ugly truth about risk managers' attitudes toward geopolitical risk is that they are amoral in their assessment of the effects on business activities.

For instance, if we consider the death toll in the civil war in Syria, estimated to "exceed 400,000, or the Rwandan Genocide during which an estimated 500,000–1,000,000 Rwandans were killed in a 100-day period, markets have been largely unaffected. I do not wish to imply that investors as individuals are not deeply affected by these tragedies. However, the narrow part of our conscience we use as investors is focused on the impact to the revenue and profits of the corporations we invest in, not the loss of life, injury or dangerous living conditions people affected by the tragedy are enduring."[36]

Most companies, whether financial institutions, corporations, or government agencies, did not allocate meaningful resources to fat TRM and lack the vision to adopt a holistic approach, which would embed, for instance, country and geopolitical risk into an investment and lending process. Geofinance is a seldom-used concept that marries geography in its broadest sense with the financial markets. In other words, it investigates the landscape of financial geography from a risk management perspective:

- A study of the influence of such factors as geography, geopolitics, economics, and demography on the financial markets, especially international financial markets, and how it affects financial risk management decisions
- A firm or governmental policy guided by geofinance
- A combination of financial, geopolitical, and geographic factors relating to risk management

UNDERSTANDING GEOFINANCIAL TAIL RISK

Considering the current state of global markets (both financial and geopolitical), one must assume that geofinancial risks will further increase in the near future. Already, a rise of geofinancial risks can be observed in regions and countries that business entrepreneurs did not think about before the financial crisis, such as Latin America (Venezuela, Cuba, Brazil,

36 C. Moore, "Geopolitical Risk—The Fear and Reality for Financial Markets," March 2015, https://www.columbiathreadneedleus.com/content/columbia/pdf/GEOPOLITICAL.PDF.

and Mexico), Asia (China, Thailand, Cambodia, and Japan), the Middle East (Turkey, Lebanon, Syria, Egypt, Libya, and Tunisia), and Africa (South Africa, the Central African Republic, Congo, and Mali).

These events now have a severe effect on financial markets with risk assets selling off sharply, on foreign exchange rates becoming volatile, and on safe-havens, such as gold, While market observers claim that until recently, financial markets have proved resilient to bursts of geo-financial volatility and uncertainty, current events in both Western and emerging markets suggest business entrepreneurs need to be more risk aware about pricing regarding geofinancial risk. In addition, this means that safe-haven assets, such as the US dollar, could see greater demand.

Tail Risk Measurement

Qualitative Identification of Tail Risks

RISK MAPPING

The notion of risk mapping is borrowed from the US agency FEMA (Federal Emergency Management Agency) but is also used within the scope of enterprise risk management.

An interesting definition of risk map comes from the CGMA (Chartered Global Management Accountant): "A risk (heat) map is a tool used to present the results of a risk assessment process visually and in a meaningful and concise way. Whether conducted as part of a broad-based enterprise risk management process or more narrowly focused internal control process, risk assessment is a critical step in risk management. It involves evaluating the likelihood and potential impact of identified risks."[37]

The CGMA continues,

> Risk maps are a way of representing the resulting qualitative and quantitative evaluations of the probability of risk occurrence and the impact on the organization in the event that a particular risk is experienced. The development of an effective risk map has several critical elements—a common understanding of the risk appetite of the company, the level of impact that would be material to

37 S. McKay, *Risk assessment for mid-sized companies: Tools for Developing a Tailored Approach to Risk Management*, Durham, NC: AICPA, 2011..

the company, and a common language for assigning probabilities and potential impacts.

To put it differently, a risk map is a data visualization tool for communicating the specific risks an organization faces. The goal of a risk map is to improve an organization's understanding of its risk profile and appetite, to clarify its thinking on the nature and impact of risks, and to improve the organization's risk assessment model. In the enterprise, a risk map is often presented as a matrix. For example, the likelihood a risk will occur may be plotted on the *X*-axis, while the impact of the same risk is plotted on the *Y*-axis.

See Cox's risk matrix theorem below.

Probability ↑			
	Low	Medium	High
	Low	Medium	Medium
	Low	Low	Low
		Impact →	

"If the organization is dispersed geographically and certain risks are associated with certain geographical areas, the risks might be illustrated with a heat map, using color to illustrate the levels of risk" to which individual branch offices are exposed.[38] One could make an inventory of the following risks:

38 M. Rouse, "What Is Risk Map?," WhatIs.com, November 2013 http://searchcompliance.techtarget.com/definition/risk-map.

- Credit risk
- Market price risks, including interest rate risk, currency risk, commodity risk, etc.
- Liquidity risk
- Funding risk
- Operational risk
- Legal and reputation risk

However, this risk map does not align well with the concept of tail risk, whereby an extreme event would take place under a low-probability scenario and would have a severe impact. Therefore, the following map would be a better reflection of the existence of tail risks.

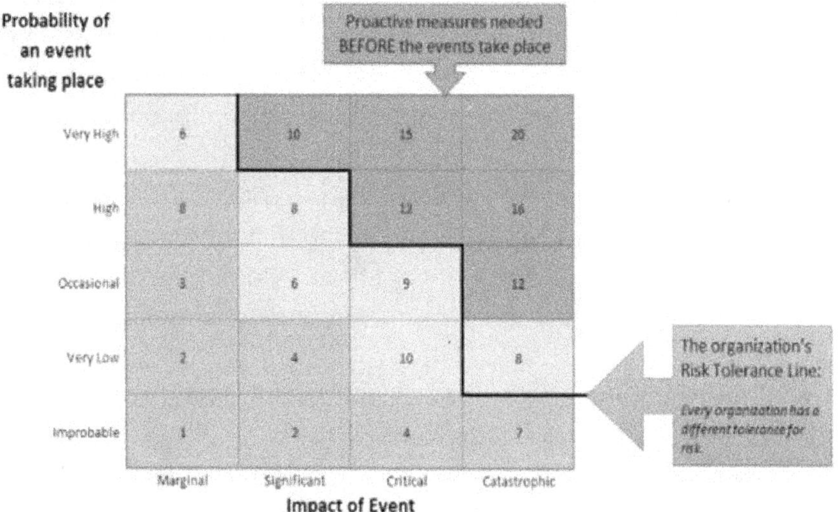

From DefCon Cyber "What's in Your Profile," https://rofori.wordpress.com/tag/nist-cybersecurity-framework/

"Above graph analyzes the operating environment of the firm to discern likelihood and impact of financial and business events. In practice, you should take the firm's prioritized list of threats and weaknesses and for each one, add a score value (1 to 10) of the probability of the event taking place, and then a score for the impact of the event. You can create a risk map (heat map) that plots the events and identifies the threats and weaknesses where you need to take proactive action to prevent or mitigate threats."[39]

In other words, risk mapping is a vulnerability analysis; the idea is to track developments for a wide variety of markets and industries, using information on both prices and quantities to spot pressure points in the firm as early as possible.

What data do we need to build a risk map (Cecchetti,2010)?

- Quantities: Simple aggregate statistics go far toward conveying a broad sense of the buildup of risks. However, to move beyond leading indicators to more sophisticated measures of systemic risk, more and better quality data are essential. We see an immediate need for information on the extent of the financial institution's exposures with respect to its peers and its participation in various markets.
- Consolidated data: Many data sets suffer from the fact that they are entirely residency-based (meaning that for globally operating firms, a local regulator might not have a view of the performances of the group in the other countries), and so consolidated figures are key.
- Consistent and comparable data: Look for data that goes across business lines and entities (subsidiaries).
- Weak spots: Identify the weakest spot and most pressing issue in each business line but also the one that has a very low probability but high severity.

The following are some sample questions to consider when implementing a risk map: (1) How much risk are we willing to accept? (2) What constitutes a material risk to our company? (3) What is the range of acceptable

39 "NIST Cybersecurity Framework," DEFCON CYBER, https://rofori.wordpress.com/tag/nist-cybersecurity-framework/.

variance from our key performance and operating metrics? (4) "How will we define our terms to evaluate the likelihood of risk events and the impact that they might have on our business, so that we can map our potential risk events to our heat map?"[40]

This exercise needs to be done once a year at the level of each business line or division within your firm. It helps senior management gain oversight on the most pressing and systemic issues that could endanger the existence of the firm.

Note: In the academic world, there is also a concept of risk map in relation to the validation of back testing methods for risk models. This three-dimensional map summarizes all the information about the performance of a risk model by reporting the *p*-value of the statistical test (the idea being to plot the number and the magnitude of the VaR exceptions). This study was conducted jointly by Gilbert Colletaz, Christophe Hurlin, and Christophe Perignon in October 2012 ("The Risk Map: A New Tool for Validating Risk Models"). But the risk map in this context is used to back test the performance of risk models and not to help a firm conduct an exhaustive risk assessment. So, I will not further elaborate on this topic—but I just wanted to mention it for the sake of completeness.

RISK SCENARIO

Risk scenario building ,is broadly defined as a process of analyzing possible future stress events by considering alternative possible outcomes (sometimes called "alternative worlds"[41]). Thus, scenario analysis, which is one of the main forms of projection, does not try to show one exact picture of the future.

The historical stress scenario analysis is a perfectly suited approach for TRM, as tail risks are defined as extreme risks that would have a catastrophic impact on an organization—in other words, those that would take place under a worst-case scenario.

---

40 S. McKay, "Risk assessment for mid-sized companies: Tools for Developing a Tailored Approach to Risk Management", Durham, NC: AICPA, 2011.

41 Madiallo, H. "Strategic Management Plan Flashcards," Quizlet, accessed April 3, 2017, https://quizlet.com/52254636/strategic-management-plan-flash-cards/.

I will once more refer to Nassim Taleb's thesis in his book *The Black Swan*, namely that unknown unknowns are responsible for the "greatest societal change."[42] And Taleb states, "The worst case is far more consequential than the forecast itself." And that is why a healthy debate about tail risk—a term used to describe the extreme ends of distributions or the very low-probability, but possible, scenarios—is necessary in a world and an industry where everything has to fit a model.

A historical scenario is based on experience during an observation period, possibly triggered by a certain historical event. For example, a scenario might be developed based on the financial crisis of 2007–2009, on the 1918–1919 Spanish flu pandemic, or on the 1923 Great Kantō earthquake. A major advantage of a scenario based on a historical event is that it can be more easily understood, since the situation has occurred.

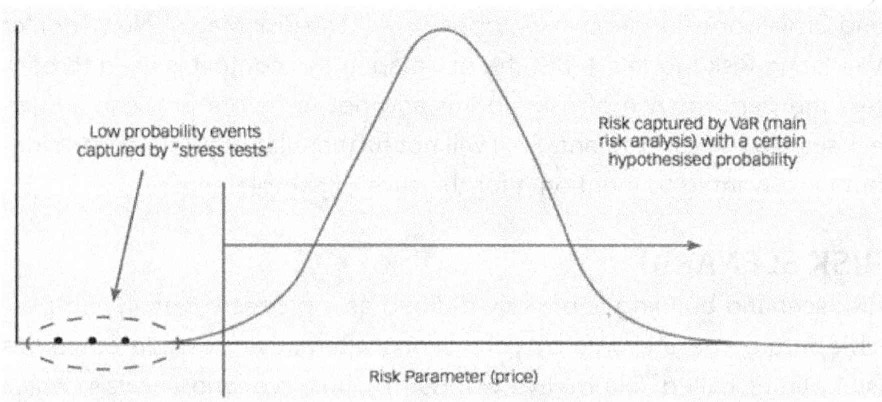

From "Stress Testing at Major Financial Institutions: Survey Results and Practice," Working Group Report, Committee on the Global Financial System, Bank for International Settlements, BASEL, Switzerland, January 2005.

And when building a forward-looking scenario, it is important to incorporate expert opinions about future world states. The forward-looking

42 Keller, C.,"Tail Risk," Gen Re Publications, accessed April 3, 2017, http://www.genre.com/knowledge/publications/tad-montross-tail-risk-en.html.

scenario analysis is a tool to explore potential weaknesses of the firm, through the interactions of (1) experts, who specify scenario shocks, (2) risk managers, who model the inferred losses, and (3) business managers, who can use the results to challenge and enhance their intuitive understanding of the behavior of their business lines in extreme scenarios.

It is worth remembering that, in the realm of financial markets, traditional risk systems assume that financial market returns are independent and identically distributed (i.i.d. or IID) and follow a normal distribution (Clauset 2011). An example of IID is the repeated tossing of a coin. We expect as many heads as tails, and the outcome of any one coin toss should be unaffected by any other.

It is well known that these models significantly underestimate the probability of so-called tail events. Although more complex models attempt to describe and simulate fat tails, these approaches are still built on the belief that one single-state distribution exists. Nowadays, it must always be remembered that the output is just an accurate mathematical articulation of expert opinion, which may itself be deeply flawed. Put more simply: garbage in, beautifully modeled garbage out.

REVERSE STRESS TESTING

As organizations seek to adapt to today's uncertain and fast-changing risk landscape, current ERM-based risk management frameworks do not provide a sound base on which to build. Indeed, current ERM frameworks are meant to be too reactive and not sufficiently anticipative or proactive.

Both financial and nonfinancial companies must "evolve and expand their existing frameworks by innovating around them"[43] and adding tools and techniques such as risk mapping, scenario modeling, predictive indicators, financial contingency planning, and reverse stress testing. I will focus here on reverse stress testing.

43 M. Armoghan, "Black Swans Turn Grey: The Transformation of Risk" PWC, accessed on April 3, 2017 http://pwc.blogs.com/files/black-swans-turn-grey-risk-practices---the-transformation-of-risk.pdf.

Now, what is reverse stress testing? In essence, "it is the process of uncovering events that, should they occur, have the potential to make your business unviable. Such events can cover credit, market and liquidity risk. It's important to remember that business failure occurs before you run out of capital. It's when counterparties are unwilling to deal with you."[44]

And, "why reverse stress test? Because it's a disciplined process of finding weaknesses in your business and deciding on the action that needs to be taken."

> "Tail risks" (low probability high loss events) are dangerous because they occur more frequently than models predict. Identifying these extreme events gives you a better chance of survival. You can decide whether you are within your risk tolerance or whether some form of action needs to be taken.
>
> How does this vary with stress testing? It is an additional risk management tool. Reverse stress testing is about plausible scenarios outside your normal stress testing requirement.[45]

Knowing the answer may help you avoid catastrophe.

In other words, these are two different ways of looking at risk. Stress testing is about applying plausible events over an economic cycle to ensure that your resources are sufficient to meet what may happen. Reverse stress testing is about identifying specific events or series of events that make your business model fail despite applying current management action. It then prompts you to ask how you can improve to reduce your vulnerability.

> Let's look at banking. What could cause your largest wholesale counterparty to fail? And what are the consequences for you? Does it tell you anything about the level of risk you currently run?

---

44 W. Webster, "Governance & Regulation," Barbican Consulting, Accessed on april 3, 2017 http://www.barbicanconsulting.co.uk/governance.

45 Ibid.

What's the role of the Board? To use its experience and understanding about the way the business works to decide on the appropriate reverse stresses, what their impact could be and whether action is required.[46]

Crucially, the ultimate responsibility for driving and embedding this change lies not with the risk function, but with the board. Its role involves building on ERM to fuse strategy more closely with risk, debate and articulate a more explicit and holistic risk appetite, and investigate collaboration to foster wider resilience across systems.

With these elements in place, the board is well equipped to embed the right risk culture and behaviours, supported by an appropriate reward structure. The resulting awareness and scrutiny of risk at all levels in every business decision will help to protect the organization's reputation—and further enhance its resilience in an uncertain world.[47]

Below is a summary:

With the growing uncertainty in the risk landscape, a technique that is being used increasingly in both the public and private sectors is "reverse stress-testing." This approach effectively accepts that it is no longer possible to forecast events themselves, and instead focuses on managing their knock-on effects or consequences.

To pick recent examples, an airline might test out the impact of most of Europe's airspace being closed down (as occurred with the volcanic eruption in Iceland), or a bank might model the effect of a major counterparty collapsing (Lehman Brothers) or a Euro member country defaulting. Reverse stress-testing is proving to

46 Ibid.

47 J. Marsh, The Actuary Newsdesk, "Risk managers unprepared for flock of black swans," January 17, 2012, http://www.theactuary.com/news/2012/01/risk-managers-unprepared-for-flock-of-black-swans/.

be a very effective way of focusing on extreme events and protecting organizations against "unknown" risks.[48]

Under the assumption that we were no longer able to either conduct proper forecasting and control of emerging risk events nor measure their impacts, what would be an appropriate approach for managing risk?"[49] In that case most organizations would be advised to build on their current ERM frameworks by making three changes to the way they frame and think about risk.

1. Developing a risk-aware culture: There is a need to move away from merely identifying, measuring, and prioritizing the various risks to the organization, "and towards a broader focus on the resilience of whole systems within which it operates and contributes value."[50] These systems include the organization's industry, political, and financial environments. This means progressing from explicit risk controls to a risk-aware culture in which risk is managed in a coordinated way across different interests, organizational units, and external relationships.
2. Explicit focus on risk appetite: The uncertainty of today's environment means that solely analyzing historical data is no longer a reliable way of predicting future events and impacts. So the board needs to be more explicit about the organization's "risk appetite in pursuing its strategy, and to build awareness at all levels of

48 M. Gotz, "Engaging Risk: Creating a Risk-Aware Culture", EY, 2016, http://www.ey.com/Publication/vwLUAssets/EY-engaging-risk-creating-a-risk-aware-culture-through-a-more-engaging-GRC-user-experience/$File/EY-engaging-risk-creating-a-risk-aware-culture-through-a-more-engaging-GRC-user-experience.pdf.

49 M. Armoghan 2011. "Black Swans Turn Grey: The Transformation of Risk." PwC, http://pwc.blogs.com/files/black-swans-turn-grey-risk-practices---the-transformation-of-risk.pdf.

50 M. Gotz, "Engaging Risk: Creating a Risk-Aware Culture", EY, 2016, http://www.ey.com/Publication/vwLUAssets/EY-engaging-risk-creating-a-risk-aware-culture-through-a-more-engaging-GRC-user-experience/$File/EY-engaging-risk-creating-a-risk-aware-culture-through-a-more-engaging-GRC-user-experience.pdf.

what risks it is willing to bear. Some employees may regard risk management as someone else's problem and a distraction from their day job. In fact, it must become part of everybody's job, every day. Also, many non-executives voice frustration that the executives on their boards are too cautious in terms of risk—so greater clarity on risk appetite would aid board effectiveness."[51]

3. Alignment of risk and strategy: There should be a parallel drive to integrate risk and strategy and to embed a risk-aware culture, behaviors, "and beliefs at all levels. Ideally, both of these strands will be led and championed by the Chief Strategy and/or Chief Risk Officer or equivalent, who should report directly to the CEO and even in some cases have a seat on the main board—a structure that is all too rare outside the financial services sector. Having the risk agenda represented at board level will also help to remove barriers traditionally placed between financial, operational and strategic risk, and encourage a more holistic view."[52]

In combination, these actions should help the organization realize four important benefits that will help it progress from managing specific risks to achieving wider resilience to risk events. These benefits are as follows[53]:

- A holistic and flexible perspective on risk and uncertainty, and an approach for managing them that is more closely integrated with the business strategy—and that recognizes that the organization's risks are constantly changing.
- Clearer ownership of risks at leadership levels—with risk awareness and accountability shared across the organization through a common risk culture.
- A greater ability to influence and shape personal behavior, as even the biggest global corporations are now critically exposed

51 Ibid.

52 Ibid.

53 Ibid.

to the actions of any individual employee anywhere in the world. As such, enhanced risk ownership, awareness, and culture help organizations manage this exposure.

- A higher market rating. There's growing evidence that businesses that are seen to truly embed a risk-aware culture and behaviors are valued more highly by the markets—enjoying a rating premium of up to 20 percent.

By evolving and expanding their risk management frameworks, organizations can achieve wider resilience to unforeseen events.

RISK STRATEGY AND APPETITE

With recent advances in financial mathematics and computational capability, progressive and complex models have been created to assist in the management of risk. At the same time, regulators, rating agencies, and capital markets have put more attention on risk controls of financial firms.

Those factors, however, did not prevent financial companies from going bankrupt or needing a government bailout in the aftermath of the GFC.

> Most of the defaulted financial firms stated they had good risk management policies and implementation and the resources spent on risk management were not trivial.
>
> The firms failed for different reasons but clearly their "good risk management" went wrong. Without a clear understanding of the risks of their business, decision makers adopted risky strategic plans. Advanced risk management models and stress testing may help with assessing the quantitative impact of risks, but understanding the company's core competence and the risks before taking them is far more important. It is critical to have clear answers to the following questions before making decisions:
>
> - What is the company's competence in the market?

- Are the decision makers familiar with the risks involved including the tail risks and understand their potential impact?
- Is the company capable of surviving extreme events?

> Risk appetite articulates the level of risk a company is prepared to accept to achieve its strategic objectives. Risk appetite frameworks help management understand a company's risk profile, find an optimal balance between risk and return, and nurture a healthy risk culture in the organization. It explains the risk tolerance of the company both qualitatively and quantitatively. Qualitative measures specify major business strategies and business goals that set up the direction of the business and outline favorable risks. Quantitative measures provide concrete levels of risk tolerance and risk limits, critical in implementing effective risk management.
>
> Risk appetite represents the willingness and the ability to take risk. Due to the sophisticated nature of financial institutions, it requires a lot of effort to fully understand the constraints and the ability to assume risk. Therefore, it is a gradual cognitive process to be updated from time to time if you enter new markets, new business and have new understanding of risks assumed.[54]

Therefore, the firm needs to establish its risk appetite or its risk strategy, or even more narrowly defined: how much tail risk is the firm willing to take on its books? In other words, how much damage to the business is the firm's senior leadership willing to suffer, expressed as a percentage of the equity that the firm can tolerate losing?

> Risk appetite has been playing a more important role in systematically determining an institution's level of risk tolerance and influencing its strategic planning. Similar to the risk objective in an investment policy statement for individual investors, risk appetite

54 K. Shang, "Risk Appetite: Linkage with Strategic Planning," Society of Actuaries, 2012,http://www.actuarialpost.co.uk/article/risk-appetite:--linkage-with-strategic-pl.

is used in different areas of strategic planning to better facilitate the analysis of risk versus return and improve decision-making. With both quantitative and qualitative analysis of the company's risk profile, risk appetite provides a holistic picture for investors and senior management.[55]

SUPPLY CHAIN RISK MANAGEMENT

Financial market players, be they financial institutions (e.g., banks, insurance companies, asset managers, and brokers) or prudential authorities, could learn a lot from how the corporate world copes with the risk management of disruptive events (we have operational risk management, but that only covers part of the problem), and supply chain risk management is one such area.

Indeed, the risk management of a front-to-back processing is missing for all financial activities. Some financing areas have adopted this process, such as treasury or trade finance, but traditional lending activities, such as corporate banking, retail banking, and institutional banking, still operate in silo architectures and lack integrity of operations.

But the importance of supply chain risk management comes particularly to light when one considers the growing importance of vendors as suppliers of services for financial firms (consulting bureaus, software companies, legal practices, etc.). As many financial firms are reducing headcounts, they are instead relying more and more on third-party providers for supplying a vast array of services and products to them.

Supply chain risk management will not only map the workflow and identify the potential risks alongside the chain within the financial firm, but it will also assess the risks related to hiring third-party providers. When an enterprise outsources business processes to an external vendor, sensitive data may be transmitted, stored, and processed on both company and vendor networks. In the United States, regulations such as the Sarbanes–Oxley Act (SOX), "Payment Card Industry Data Security Standard (PCI

55 M. Neumann, "Risk Appetite: Linkage Between Risk Appetite and Strategic Planning," ERM Symposium, Washington DC, April 2012.

DSS) and the Health Information Portability and Accountability Act (HIPAA) mandate that risk management policies extend to third-party vendors, outsourcers, contractors and consultants."[56]

To illustrate how supply chains also affect financial firms, the flowchart below highlights an example of a chain of operations in relation to the issuance of a letter of credit.

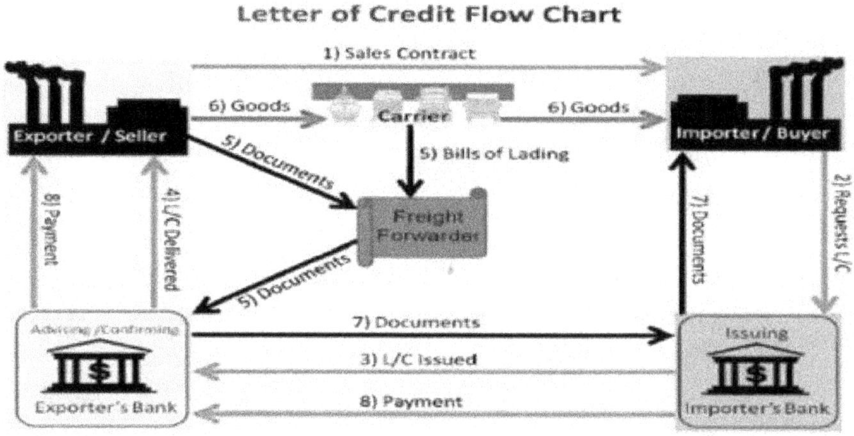

From Agri-Exchange.[57]

In an ideal world, within such a financial firm, the workflow of the sales desk should be integrated with the middle office, risk management, back office (in relation to settlement and confirmation), accounting, reporting, and enquiries. A simple proof of this segregation is the mere existence of different IT architectures and software for each of those activities lacking efficient bridges among these areas of operations.

> Going back to the corporate world, traditional methods for managing supply chain risk rely on knowing the likelihood of occurrence and the magnitude of impact for every potential event that

56 S. Patel "Vendor Assurance," CloudeAssurance, accessed on April 3, 2017 https://www.cloudeassurance.com/services/vendor-assurance/.

57 K. Sudhanshu "Letter of Credit Flow Chart," accessed May 4, 2017, http://agriexchange.apeda.gov.in/Ready%20Reckoner/LETTER_OF_CREDIT.aspx.

> could materially disrupt a firm's operations. For common supply-chain disruptions—poor supplier performance, forecast errors, transportation breakdowns, and so on—those methods work very well, using historical data to quantify the level of risk.
>
> But it's a different story for low-probability, high-impact events—megadisasters like Hurricane Katrina in 2005, viral epidemics like the 2003 SARS outbreak, or major outages due to unforeseen events such as factory fires and political upheavals. Because historical data on these rare events are limited or nonexistent, their risk is hard to quantify using traditional models. As a result, many companies do not adequately prepare for cases of disruptive events. That can have calamitous consequences when catastrophes do strike and can force even operationally savvy companies to scramble after the fact—think of Toyota following the 2011 Fukushima earthquake and tsunami.[58]

To address this challenge, instead of developing a financial model that focuses on determining the probability that any specific risk will occur, an alternative is to focus on the description of the supply chain that emphasizes the effect of potential failures at points along the supply chain (such as the closing of a supplier's factory or a flood at a distribution center), rather than on the cause of the disruption. This type of analysis obviates the need to determine the probability that any specific risk will occur—a valid approach because the mitigation strategies for a disruption are equally effective regardless of what caused it.

Using this approach, companies can quantify what the financial and operational effects would be if a critical supplier's facility were out of commission for, say, two weeks—whatever the reason. The computerized model can be updated easily and quickly, which is crucial because supply chains are in a continual state of flux. A central characteristic of this

58 D. Simchi-Levi, "From Superstorms to Factory Fires: Managing Unpredictable," *Harvard Business Review*, 2014, https://hbr.org/2014/01/from-superstorms-to-factory-fires-managing-unpredictable-supply-chain-disruptions.

approach is the time to recovery (TTR), namely, the time it would take for a particular node (such as a supplier facility, a distribution center, or a transportation hub) to be restored to full functionality after a disruption. Examining historical experience and surveying the firm's buyers or suppliers determine the TTR values.

To conduct the analysis, the approach removes one node at a time from the supply network for the duration of the TTR. It then determines the supply chain response that would minimize the performance effect of the disruption at that node—for instance, drawing down inventory, shifting production, expediting transportation, or reallocating resources.

Based on the optimal response, it generates a financial or operational performance impact (PI) for the node. A company can choose different measures of PI, such as lost units of production, revenue, or profit margin. The approach analyzes all nodes in the network, assigning a PI to each.

The node with the largest PI (in lost sales, for instance, or lost units of production) is assigned a Risk Exposure Index (REI) score of 1.0. All other nodes' REI scores are indexed relative to this value (a node whose disruption would cause the least effect receives a value close to zero). The indexed scores allow the firm to identify at a glance the nodes that should get the most attention from risk managers.

This approach provides the following benefits:

- √ Identifies hidden exposures. The approach helps managers identify which nodes in the network create the greatest risk exposure—often highlighting previously hidden or overlooked areas of high risk. It also allows the firm to compare the costs and benefits of various alternatives for mitigating impact.
- √ Avoids the need for predictions about rare events. The approach determines the optimal response to any disruption that might occur within the supply network, regardless of the cause. Rather than trying to quantify the likelihood that a low-probability, high-risk event will strike, firms can focus on identifying the most

important exposures and putting in place risk management strategies to mitigate them.

√ Reveals supply chain dependencies and bottlenecks. Companies can also use the analyses to make inventory and sourcing decisions that increase the robustness of the network. This includes considering the likely scramble among rival companies to lock in alternative sources if a supplier's disruption affects several firms. Such cross-firm effects of a crisis are often overlooked. Contracts with backup suppliers can be negotiated to give a company priority over others should a disruption with the primary supplier occur, which would decrease the TTR and financial impact.

√ Promotes discussion and learning. While analyzing the supply chain in this way, managers engage in discussions with suppliers and internal groups about acceptable levels of the TTR for critical facilities and share insight about best-practice processes to reduce recovery time. Thus, the impact of disruptions is minimized.

Therefore, it is highly useful to map the process in a way that allows a description of the front-to-back process in relation to payments, lending, investments, and so on, and to examine how a disruption would affect one of the nodes alongside the supply chain for each of these financial activities and how long it would take for the system to recover (i.e., reconduct the business as a going concern to the benefit of the customers).

Quantification of Tail Risk Events

STANDARD METHODS OF RISK QUANTIFICATION

In general, the tail means the extreme cases in a probability distribution. Tail risk in financial returns indicates the extreme losses or gains in the financial market. Popular tools for the measurement of tail risk include VaR, CoVaR or expected shortfall (ES), and the common estimation approach of VaR—the extreme value theory approach. However, I am not a fan of mathematical models, favoring instead structural qualitative solutions for TRM.

For many years, VaR has been the standard measure used for risk management. VaR is defined as the worst loss over a given holding period within a fixed confidence level. A shortcoming of the VaR is that it disregards any loss beyond the VaR level.

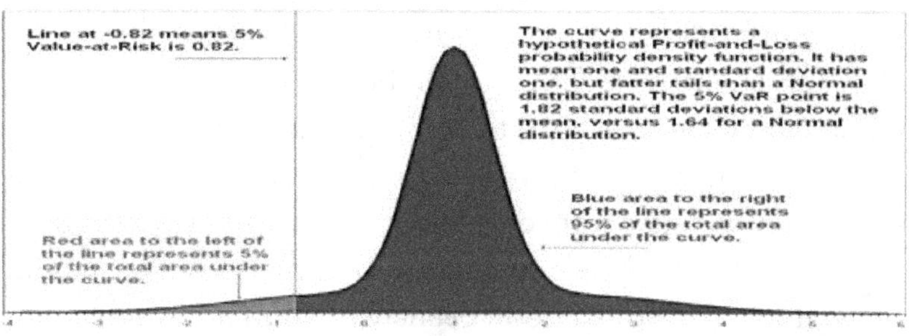

From Wikipedia.[59]

59 *Wikipedia*, s.v. "Value at Risk," accessed May 4, 2017, https://en.wikipedia.org/wiki/Value_at_risk.

ES is an alternative risk measure that addresses this issue. ES is defined as the expected loss conditional on the losses being beyond the VaR level. ES is also called expected tail loss or conditional VaR and describes the amount of loss to be expected when that loss has breached the VaR value.

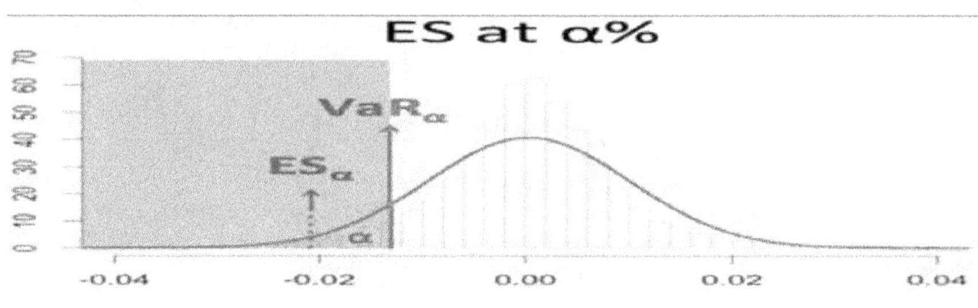

From Portfolio Mason.[60]

Another frequently used measure is Moody's KMV expected default frequency (EDF) RiskCalc model.[61] Moody's KMV is a distance-to-default measure that turns into an expected default probability with the help of a large historical data set on defaults. The distance to default is measured as the number of standard deviations by which the expected asset value exceeds the default point. A firm's one-year expected default probability is calculated as the fraction of those firms in previous years that had the same distance to default and defaulted within one year.

While these measures focus on individual bank risk, there has been a growing interest in recent years in systemic measures of bank risk. One strand of the literature focuses on tail betas. This concept applies extreme value theory (Novak 2011) to derive predictions about an individual bank's value in the event of a very large (negative) systemic shock. This method uses information from days where stock market prices have fallen heavily and considers the covariation with a bank's share price on the same day. It focuses on realized covariances conditional on large share

60 "Portfolio Mason: Definitions," accessed May 5, 2017, https://en.wikipedia.org/wiki/Value_at_risk.

61 Moody's Analytics, History of KMV.

price drops. A difficulty encountered when applying this method is that tail risk observations are rarely observed; hence, many observations are needed to obtain accurate estimates (at least six years of daily data is suggested).

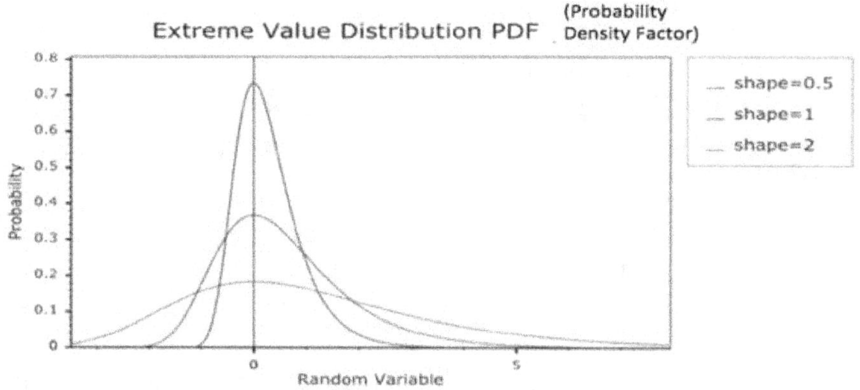

From Kotz and Nadarajah (2000).

MEASURING TAIL RISK OF FINANCIAL INSTITUTIONS VIA SHARE PRICE FLUCTUATIONS

To address the risk of systemic crises to a financial firm, it is of paramount importance to have advance information about bank exposures to large (negative) shocks. Tail risk is defined as bank exposure to a large negative market shock and is measured by estimating bank share price sensitivity to changes in far out-of-the-money put options on the market, correcting for market movements (Knaup 2010). In other words, share prices of banks will generally respond to news about the likelihood of a market crash; however, a bank with higher systemic tail exposure should react more strongly. One could identify tail exposure by the bank's sensitivity to tail risk news.

Because far out-of-the-money put options on the market only pay out if the market crashes, changes in their prices reflect changes in the perceived likelihood and severity of a crash (Knaup 2012). The estimated sensitivities, in turn, represent the market's perception of exposures to a hypothetical crash, making them a truly forward-looking measure. In other words, the way to measure tail risk at banks is by obtaining the TRM from the market regression amended by market's put-option exposure to prolonged downturn (not daily or weekly drops). The key is that it must be forward looking (i.e., the perceived exposure to future crash). Another attractive feature of this measure is that it does not require the actual observation of tail risk events, because it identifies bank tail risk exposure through changes in expected market tail risk.

Based on a study using a sample of 209 large US bank holding companies covering the period from October 2005 to September 2008 with the use of both market data (share prices, stock market index, and put options on the market) and balance sheet data, banks that appear safer in normal periods are actually more crisis prone (Knaup and Wagner 2010). The effect of nontraditional activities on tail risk depends on whether they leave assets on the balance sheets or not. In the former case, they increase tail risk, while in the latter they do not. Several nontraditional activities contribute to tail risk: for-sale securities, trading assets, and derivatives used for trading. However, securitization and asset-sale activities (where risk is transferred) are not significant. Results also suggest that leverage itself does not increase tail risk, but it will do so if it comes through uninsured deposits. Large time deposits increase tail risk, as these deposits (above $100,000) are not insured and may be withdrawn in crisis (note: now raised to $250,000).

HOW TO PRICE-IN TAIL RISKS FROM A BOND MARKET PERSPECTIVE

Until recently, at least within the European Union, the implicit bailout guarantees of financial institutions exacerbated the moral hazard in the financial markets and weakened market discipline. Indeed, the relationship between yield spreads and tail risk is significantly weaker (Chava,2014) for depository institutions, large institutions, government-sponsored entities, and politically connected institutions and in periods following large-scale bailouts of financial institutions.

The impetus to focus on the pricing of tail risk of financial institutions is because financial institutions (compared to the corporate world) are highly leveraged entities, whose equity capital may not be adequate to absorb the large losses that materialize when a tail event occurs (cf. the graph of leverage ratios for major investment banks in the period up to the start of the GFC). Given that fixed-income investors hold uninsured liabilities that do not share in the upside from tail risk but may have to absorb losses when the tail risk materializes, it is rational to expect they will demand higher yield spreads from institutions with higher tail risk exposures.

Hence, one should discuss the pricing of bonds issued by financial institutions that would be mispriced as implicit bailout guarantees, which may engender moral hazard problems among bond market investors[62] Bondholders of systemically important financial institutions may have rationally anticipated (until recently, as bail-in mechanisms are coming into play) a taxpayer-funded bailout of their institution in the event of a systemic crisis and thus may not have priced the institution's exposure to tail risk, especially systemic tail risk.

The experience of the recent financial crisis, during which bondholders of many distressed institutions could avoid losses thanks to government bailouts, lends credence to the moral hazard argument. Another reason bonds are mispriced is that investors do not really expect a large tail event, such as the financial crisis, to materialize and hence tend to ignore tail risk as a low-probability, nonsalient risk before the crisis.

LOSS, THREAT, AND VULNERABILITY ANALYSIS

There is an alternative method for considering risk; it is the very process of defining exactly *what* we are trying to protect, from *whom* we are trying to protect it, and, most importantly, *how* we are going to protect it.

62 L. Yi, "Institutional Herding and Its Price Impact: Evidence from the Corporate Bond Market" 2016-091 Federal Reserve Board, Washington D.C.

> In today's world, if you are a CEO, CRO, CFO, COO, business entrepreneur, investor, government official, or in other leadership positions that can implement change in an organization, it is crucial to maintain a diligent overview and understanding of risk, threat, and vulnerability. Many articles and blog posts attempt to define these three terms individually; however, it is the interactive relationship of all three of these components that create the initial evaluation and recommended action plan for risk management. For individuals in overseeing the risk management of an organization, the more this process can be rationalized in a way that is similar to the approach of a professional high-level risk expert, the better the individual's understanding and interpretation of the results of the risk audits as well as their ability to implement their findings in a way most suited to the company or institution.[63]

Moreover, as a reminder, this is how risk, threat, and vulnerability interact[64]:

$$\textit{Risk} = \textit{Threat} \times \textit{Vulnerability} \times \textit{Cost}$$

where

$$\textit{Cost} = \textit{Operational Costs} + \textit{Reputational Costs} + \textit{Revenue Costs}$$

Risk assessment causes one to reassess because the most valued items—the critical resources—must be protected. The initial question requiring an answer is, "What is the most critical resource, the one that would have the biggest impact if it were compromised?" That resource needs the most protection! When conducting a risk assessment, it is not uncommon

63 B. Pazderka, "Threat vs Vulnerability vs Risk: What Is the Difference?," Pinkterton, October 16, 2014 https://www.pinkerton.com/blog/risk-vs-threat-vs-vulnerability-and-why-you-shoul.

64 N. Renfroe and J. Smith, "Threat, Vulnerability Assessments and Risk Analysis," Applied Research Associates, Last Modified August 2017, https://wbdg.org/resources/threat-vulnerability-assessments-and-risk-analysis.

for an organization to have a false sense of security because they have "thrown in all sorts of security measures." Very often, there is a weakness that can be exploited, one of which the organization and their risk management team is unaware.

Risk is in essence a function of the values of threat, consequence, and vulnerability, and looking at risk through these three dimensions can help the firm build a comprehensive risk database and design a risk map accordingly. As a result of such an analysis, the matrix below shows the threat on the *y*-axis and the vulnerability of the firm on the *x*-axis.

	Risk				
Severe	H	H	C	C	C
High	M	H	H	C	C
Significant	M	M	H	H	C
Moderate	L	M	M	H	H
Low	L	L	M	M	M
Very Low	L	L	M	M	M
	VL	L	M	H	VH

From the University of Michigan.[65]

In other words, to take a step back, the objective of risk management is to create a level of protection that mitigates vulnerabilities to threats and the potential consequences, thereby reducing risk to an acceptable level.

A variety of mathematical models are available to calculate risk and illustrate the effects of increasing protective measures on the risk equation.

65 "Michigan Hazard Mitigation Plan: Risk and Vulnerability Assessments," University of Michigan, accessed May 4, 2017, http://www.michigan.gov/documents/msp/MHMP_2014_UPDATE_PART_2_RISK_AND_VULNERABILITY_ASSESSMENTS_DRAFT_449965_7.pdf.

- The first step in a risk management program is a threat assessment. A threat assessment considers the full spectrum of threats (natural, criminal, terrorist, accidental, etc.) for a given firm. The assessment should examine supporting information to evaluate the relative likelihood of occurrence for each threat.
- Once the plausible threats are identified, a vulnerability assessment must be performed. The vulnerability assessment considers the potential effects of loss from an unlikely event as well as the vulnerability of the firm to the effects of an unlikely event. The effect of loss is the degree to which the mission of the firm is impaired by the effects of the given threat.
- Vulnerability is defined as a combination of the attractiveness of a firm as a target and the level of deterrence or defense provided by the existing countermeasures or mitigation.

One needs insight into how big the consequence is, the likelihood of its occurrence, and its potential effect on the entity to undertake the process of managing risk. Risk, threat, and vulnerability are not interchangeable terms, although threat and vulnerability are a part of risk.

Here are some important characteristics of the three components:

1. Threats (effects) generally cannot be controlled. One cannot stop the efforts of an international terrorist group or prevent a hurricane or a tsunami in advance. Threats must be identified, but they often remain outside of one's control.
2. Risk can be mitigated. One can manage risk to either lower vulnerability or lower the overall effects on the business.
3. Vulnerability can be treated. One should identify weaknesses and take proactive measures to correct identified vulnerabilities.

PROBABLE MAXIMUM LOSS

The International Risk Management Institute defines the concept of probable maximum loss (PML) in the insurance industry as measuring the maximum damage if the worst happens, and all the mitigations work to reduce the effects of the damage.

PML is a term that has been borrowed from the insurance industry, the petrochemical sector, and the commercial real-estate sector.

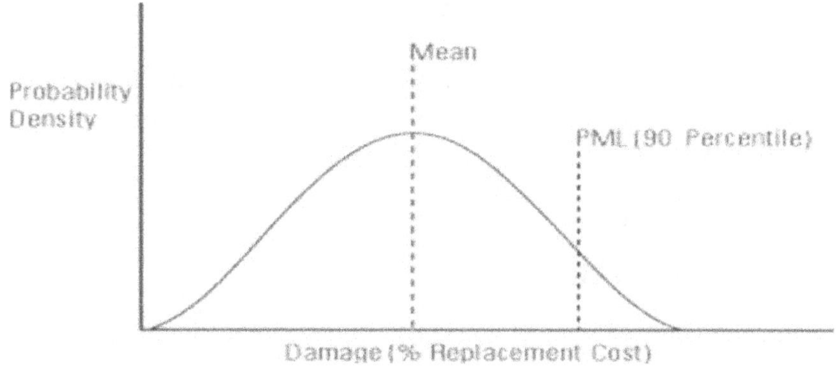

From ST-Risk.[66]

This can be adapted to measure and manage a financial firm's strength or fragility in relation to extreme risk.

If you transpose the PML concept to financial firms, you can define it as the value of the largest loss that could result from a disaster, assuming the normal functioning of passive protective features (e.g., three-line defense system with the firm, a normally functioning enterprise risk management, etc.) and proper functioning of most (perhaps not all) active suppression systems (e.g., credit committees that can take quick derisking or provisioning decisions).

PML is usually expressed as a percentage of the total value, experienced by a structure or collection of structures, when subjected to a maximum credible event. Potential exists for a firm to be financially destroyed by an extreme financial-political event peril; thus, the PML is the value of the entire firm and all the business lines.

66 "Fragilities," st-risk.com, accessed May 4, 2017, http://www.st-risk.com/tech_fragilities.html.

> However, the probability that the entire firm will financially be destroyed varies based on the protective safeguards in place as well as the collateral, derivatives, life-line shareholders, liquidity backup central bank, and reinsurance. The combination of these factors yields the estimated PML.[67]

In other words, PML is the worst-case scenario and the most pessimistic view—the entire firm and all business lines could financially be destroyed (such loss could be considered a *shock loss*). Other terms for PML are *amount subject to loss* and *maximum foreseeable loss*.

EARNINGS AT RISK AND CASH FLOW AT RISK

Your firm needs a measure of the risk associated with structural asset exposures that cannot easily be closed out, such as illiquid assets held on the balance sheet of a financial firm.

Now, as you may know, commercial insurance underwriters and insurance companies alike use probable maximum loss (PML) calculations to estimate the highest maximum claim that a business most likely will file, versus what it could file, for damages resulting from a catastrophic event. Although underwriters use complex statistical formulas and frequency distribution charts, the concepts involved are not difficult to understand. In fact, once you understand the basic formula, you can estimate your own PML and use this information as a starting point in negotiating favorable commercial insurance rates.

At the end of the day, probable maximum loss has a lot of similarities with earnings or cash flow at risk (EaR or CaR), as these are variables that are being used for structural nonspeculative assets. EaR (CaR) measurement is more diagnostic, focused on understanding the complex interaction between physical assets and hedges under different market outcomes. However, no degree of sophistication of "at risk" calculation is

67 D. Stokes, "Energy Risk Management: The Demise of Value at Risk," Timera Energy, March 19, 2012 http://www.timera-energy.com/energy-risk-management-the-demise-of-value-at-risk/.

a substitute for developing complementary risk measures. An effectively implemented stress test framework is an invaluable tool for understanding the impacts of extreme risks.

Therefore, eHow contributor Jackie Lohrey proposes five steps for easily calculating your own earnings that might be at risk in case of an extreme event[68]:

- "Calculate the dollar value of business investment to establish the amount you stand to lose if a catastrophic event demolished your investment project. If you already have business insurance, this is the amount of insurance coverage. Otherwise, add real property and business personal property to reach the valuation.
- "Identify risk factors that increase the chance a specific catastrophic event would demolish your business. You can use a risk mapping technique where you flag all possible risks—including those low probability-high severity events. For example, risks associated with exchange rate or interest rate fluctuations, a dispute in the South and/or East China Sea, a deep dive into recession of the European Union, a spike in oil prices because of rising insecurity in the Middle East, your most important client or vendor going bankrupt, etc.
- "Identify risk mitigation factors that decrease the chance a specific catastrophic event would demolish your business. For example, risk mitigation factors associated with an exchange and/or interest rate fluctuations can be mitigated through swaps, a dispute in a geographic zone can be partially covered through a trade credit insurance, a client's risk can be hedged through an offtaker's agreement, a non-delivery risk can be insured through a supplier credit insurance. Also, consider elements in your scenario analysis such as for example a better client/supplier diversification.

68 J. Lohrey, "How to Calculate Probable Maximum Loss," eHow, accessed on April 4, 2017 http://www.ehow.com/how_8743379_calculate-probable-maximum-loss.html.

- "Conduct a (reverse stress testing) scenario analysis to estimate the degree to which risk mitigation factors decrease the chance an extreme event will demolish your business. Again, an effectively implemented stress test framework is an invaluable tool for understanding the impacts of extreme risks. The difference between these two factors determines the maximum loss your business is likely to incur. Insurance companies typically use percentages that increase incrementally by 1%. For example, an analysis might determine that risk mitigation decreases the chance of a total loss by 21%.
- "Multiply the investment valuation by the highest expected loss percentage to calculate the probable maximum loss. For example, if the investment valuation is $500,000 and you determine that risk mitigation reduces expected losses by 20%, probable maximum loss for a fire is $500,000 multiplied by .80 or $400,000."

On an ongoing basis, your firm needs to build an early-warning system that accounts for those risks you have flagged and monitor them onward. However, be flexible and alert enough to adjust the nature of those red flags as well their triggers. It is also key to gain understanding from analyzing the interaction between portfolio exposures and risk factors.

TIME TO RECOVERY

The time to recovery (TTR) is used in the supply chain risk management realm and addresses the way to identify the weakest link in the supply chain. TTR is defined as the time it takes for a supply chain node to fully recover after a disruption. The reason managers need to know TTR is so they can plan for completely unexpected events. These could be funding-related events, geopolitical crises, a Chinese market crash, or other reasons that would shut down a firm financially, rendering it unable to function for an extended period.

The TTR may be close to zero if the firm has an alternative plan that can take over, preferably in another region with enough inventory to enable survival through the break, or other backup plans. However, to mitigate risk, managers need to know what these are and ensure there are no problems with second- and third-tier suppliers as well. Knowing the TTR, one can better manage unpredictable supply chain disruptions, as it helps prioritize the financial impact of risk through the Risk Exposure Index (REI). "Risk Exposure Index™ enables companies for the first time to fully quantify their maximum risk exposure from natural disasters or any other unpredictable supply chain disruptions. It specifically assesses for each node, or site, in a given supply chain the resulting financial impact, such as loss of revenue or loss of profit, or operational impact, such as loss of production volume."[69] This in turn enables companies to focus their mitigation efforts on the most important suppliers and risk areas instead of ignoring them or using an exhaustive approach. Ford Motor Company successfully applied this method (Simchi-Levi 2015).

By removing one node at a time and calculating the response (draw-down from inventory, alternate suppliers, etc.), we can calculate the financial impact of the loss of the node. The financial impact of all nodes is then used to create the REI, which enables prioritization of risk mitigation based on the most critical areas of the supply chain. These are not always those that are expected. In the Ford case, many of the suppliers were of low cost spent but were nevertheless critical.

69 "Risk Exposure Index™ (REI)," MIT Forum for Supply Chain, http://supplychain.mit.edu/2015/03/rei/.

Tail Risk Response

Tail Risk Management Is Much More Than Merely Tail Hedging

QUANTITATIVE TAIL RISK PROTECTION STRATEGIES

TRM is much more than merely hedging; it is more about solid portfolio risk management skills that embody just-in-case risk management. TRM is also much more than shielding asset returns from unexpected events. TRM is about protecting the firm or fund capital from sudden massive losses and providing sustainability. Hedging clearly focuses on managing price risk or striking a balance between uncertainty and the risk of opportunity loss. It aims to shield the sensitivity of the core business of a firm from the sensitivity to movements in financial prices.

"Protecting against tail events can help improve long-term performance for even well-diversified investors seeking to capture premia from risky assets."[70] In other words, "protection during periods of market distress allows managers to reallocate to riskier assets in the aftermath of the event,"[71] just when the expected returns are the highest. There are four methods for controlling tail risk: (1) long volatility, (2) low-volatility equity,

70 "Equity Market Risk: Getting The Big One Right," State Street Global Advisors, https://www.ssga.com/investment-topics/equity/gmo-2015-equity-market-risk-getting-the-big-one-right.pdf.

71 R. Benson, R. K. Shapiro, D. Smith, and R. Thomas, "A Comparison of Tail Risk Protection Strategies in the U.S.," *Alternative Investment Analyst Review*, 2011, https://www.caia.org/sites/default/files/2013-aiar-q1-comparison.pdf.

(3) trend following, and (4) equity exposure management (Akoundi and Haugh 2010).

According to prevalent hedge fund industry practices (Asness, Krail, and Liew 2001, 6–19), the ideal tail risk strategy combines a low-performance drag with a high certainty of protection. One can consider an investment strategy to offer tail risk protection if it consistently outperforms equities when equity returns are most negative. One can define portfolio tail risk as the conditional mean portfolio return in months where equity returns exceed a loss of 5 percent (Benson, Shapiro, Smith, and Thomas 2011). For each tail risk strategy, one can estimate the fixed allocation, which, "when combined with an equity portfolio, reduces tail risk by a constant proportion. In this way, each tail risk strategy is compared on an equal footing based on its contribution to tail risk reduction. Good tail risk protection may benefit portfolios in several ways"[72]:

- √ Tail risk hedging can boost total portfolio profitability because a hedged portfolio allows for a more growth-oriented asset allocation.
- √ Tail risk has a significant, positive relationship with forward expected returns.

CHALLENGES IN TAIL RISK HEDGING[73]

- √ Fewer market participants to sell options. "Buying put options is currently the most popular form of tail risk hedging. Despite the growing demand to buy long-term put options from both institutional and individual investors," fewer market participants are willing or able to sell these options. Whereas an option buyer's risk is limited to the premium he or she pays, an option seller has much greater risk (Gerstei 2012).

---

72 Ibid.

73 A. Gerstein, "The Challenges in Hedging Tail Risk," *New York Times*, April 20, 2012 https://dealbook.nytimes.com/2012/04/20/the-challenges-in-hedging-tail-risk/.

- √ With the Volcker rule, which seeks to reduce excessive risk at banks, banks not only need to decrease the amount of long-dated options they sell, but they must also increase the amount of collateral required for these trades, further limiting the number of option sellers.
- √ The increased demand to buy put options (which are priced in terms of implied volatility), coupled with a lack of people willing and able to sell them, has led to excessively high-volatility prices, especially in longer-dated maturities. With the increase in price volatility, the cost of portfolio protection has also increased, causing prospective hedgers to often overpay for this insurance.
- √ The cost of tail risk hedging represents a constant drag on returns, preventing targeted returns from being met.
- √ From a pure investment perspective, while diversifying among asset classes with low correlation might sound like a good tool to hedge against tail risk, simply diversifying global equity with fixed income, for example, does not do enough to limit that tail risk given that in times of crisis correlations tend to rise, as shown in the table below.

Normal

	S&P500
S&P500	1.00
Russell2000	0.70
MSCI World x US	0.61
MSCI EM	0.54
US Aggregate	0.18
High Yield	0.51
S&P GSCI	0.02
FTSE NAREIT	0.42
HFRI Fund Weighted	0.60

Crisis

	S&P500
S&P500	1.00
Russell2000	0.75
MSCI World x US	0.77
MSCI EM	0.73
US Aggregate	0.34
High Yield	0.75
S&P GSCI	0.46
FTSE NAREIT	0.66
HFRI Fund Weighted	0.71

Crisis - Normal

	S&P500
S&P500	1.00
Russell2000	0.05
MSCI World x US	0.16
MSCI EM	0.19
US Aggregate	0.15
High Yield	0.23
S&P GSCI	0.43
FTSE NAREIT	0.25
HFRI Fund Weighted	0.11

From Chartered Alternative Investment Analyst Association.[74]

---

74 R. Benson, R. Shapiro, and R. Thomas, "A Comparison of Tail Risk Protection Strategies in the U.S. Market," accessed May 4, 2017, https://www.caia.org/sites/default/files/2013-aiar-q1-comparison.pdf.

WHAT IT MEANS TO BUILD AN EFFECTIVE TAIL RISK DEFENSE

Almost anyone familiar with the saga of the Basel III response to the GFC will agree that the regulators have not addressed the cause of "the fundamental risk management failure"; instead, they merely focused on the symptoms of the crisis (i.e., depressed asset prices, reduced liquidity in many markets, and a contraction in the credit markets) by steering toward the creation of a stronger loss absorption capability and higher liquidity. "The danger is that, by the time the industry completes the Basel III implementation in 2018, it will only be fully prepared for the 2008 crisis"[75]—and even that is far from the truth. This would neither be adequate nor prepare the industry for changes that would have developed in that time. Therefore, financial firms must emphasize the definition and implementation of a TRM framework that is proactively identified and effectively mitigates extreme risk events regardless of the crisis scenario.

The classic risk management framework was built to deal with normal risk (under a standard normal assumption, the bell curve) and has often failed to provide an effective response when a tail risk event has unfolded. That is because, unlike "normal" risk, tail risk often comes unmeasured and unpredicted, stemming from the unknown unknowns. The existing risk management framework needs to be enhanced and concomitantly brought back to basics; it is essential to have a custom-built TRM architecture, which should include three lines of tail risk defense[76]:

- Focus on a firm's business strategy and model. The analysis of the financial firm failures suggests that flawed business strategies or models appear to be the prime causes of fiascos. It is necessary to set up an approach to examine a firm's strategies and to diagnose the areas outside its comfort zone where it is exposed to extreme unmanageable risk. To optimize strategy, the risk appetite should

75 Risk Management Events, "Effective Tail Risk Management versus Excessive Protection," RME, PRMIA, 2013, https://prmiadc.wordpress.com/themes/governance/effective-tail-risk-management-v.

76 Ibid.

be set correctly. The key role of risk appetite is to optimize a firm's exposure to tail risk by striking the right balance between businesses the firm will run inside and outside of its comfort zone.

- The day-to-day risk management practice must identify any potential tail risk events when they are largely invisible or look like a remote threat. The firm should create early-warning signal tools, focusing both on conventional risk and on (extreme) tail risk. Another principal method is scenario and stress testing with a strong emphasis on reverse stress testing. There is no novelty in using stress testing, but stress testing tail risk scenarios is special. Traditional number crunching does not work here. Instead, the focus is on the thinking process concerning "what if" and detailed contingency planning, similar to business continuity planning (BCP) undertaken for mitigating operational risks. If scenario testing is done properly, it becomes a sort of a flight simulator for training people to manage tail risk. Even very conservative firms are not immune to tail risk crises.
- Mitigate the effects if such a crisis does occur. The skills of driving through the crisis determine the ability of a firm to survive it. The robust tail risk crisis mitigation framework should include effective crisis alerts, multilevel contingency plans, IT infrastructure and reporting adapted for tail risk, effective crisis governance, and a proactive communication approach.

As already highlighted several times, it is important to emphasize that capital management is not the same as TRM. While capital management aims to allocate economic capital in the most efficient and strategic way by considering risk-weighted assets, cost of carry, and so on, TRM goes a step further. It looks at preserving the capital in the event of an extreme risk occurring, or in other words, it operates as just-in-case risk management.

"Nowadays, ERM is frequently discussed. ERM indeed intends to provide an integrated, comprehensive assessment of all the risks that an institution is exposed to and an objective and consistent approach to managing them."[77] Tail risk management involves one of those risks that must be integrated.

Every firm should behave in such a manner in relation to risk management. Unfortunately, seven years after the Lehman Brothers collapse, we still run the risk of "wasting a good crisis." We have already paid too high a price for neglecting the importance of TRM. While regulators focus on macroprudential instruments for battling the symptoms of the crisis, the real cause remains unaddressed. Implementation of a robust TRM practice is paramount not only to the survival of a single firm but also for the stability of the entire financial sector, and even beyond the economic system.

77 J. Ribiero, "Global Risk Management Survey: Sixth Edition Risk—Risk Management in the Spotlight," Deloitte, 2010, http://www.ucop.edu/enterprise-risk-management/_files/deloitte_globalrskmgtsrvy.pdf.

Tail Risk Portfolio Management

HOW NORMALLY UNCORRELATED MARKETS BECOME CORRELATED

"Under what is known as modern portfolio theory, you can reduce the overall risk in an investment portfolio and even boost your overall returns by investing in asset combinations that are not correlated,"[78] or in other words by diversifying your portfolio. Uncorrelated assets don't tend to move in the same way at the same time. If there is zero correlation or negative or noncorrelation, one asset will go up when the other is down, and vice versa.

> Consequently, cautious investors typically building portfolios that include asset classes that have low correlation—the measure of the strength of the linear relationship between two variables.
>
> Values can range from +1.00 (perfect correlation) to –1.00 (perfect negative correlation). Two assets are positively correlated means that when one asset produces above average returns, the other tends to also produce above average returns. Conversely, negative correlation means that when one produces above average returns, the other tends to produce below average returns.

---

78 M. Phipps, "What Are Correlated and Non-Correlated Assets?," The Balance, 2016, https://www.thebalance.com/what-is-asset-correlation-2894312.

> Thus, the lower the correlation of returns, the more effective the asset class is as a diversifier of portfolio risk.[79]

The problem for investors is that they fail to understand that correlations are not stable—they drift. And while international stocks and emerging market stocks are exposed to some different economic and political risks than are Western-based stocks (United States, Europe, Japan, Australia, New Zealand, and Canada), "they are also exposed to some of the same risks that can impact the global economy. And when those risks show up (typically during times of financial and/or political crises), correlations among all asset classes tend to turn high. Just when the benefits of diversification are needed most, they go AWOL."[80]

Two asset classes could previously have been uncorrelated but can suddenly become correlated, as investors become risk averse during stressed markets and even prefer to forego profit opportunities.

Under normal circumstances, commodities are weakly correlated with stocks and bonds and positively correlated with inflation. When stocks rise, commodities fall. However, in 2008, commodity investors also looked for risk-free assets—treasuries. Commodity prices fell in parallel with stocks and nontreasury bonds. Correlations also work as expected in a normal market because more lenders are willing to lend, and more investors are ready to borrow and participate in the market (Rankin and Idil 2014).

In stressed markets, fewer lenders are ready to lend money and instead try to withdraw loans. As a result, investors sell both performing and nonperforming assets, which results in reduced market participation and increased correlation among asset prices. Therefore, the correlation risk is directly proportional to liquidity and is procyclical. It is important that investors understand that correlations are not static—they do drift. And correlations are likely to rise to very high levels during times of crisis.

79 L. Swedroe, "Correlation of Returns: The Reason Why Diversification Didn't Work," Moolanomy, 2009, http://www.moolanomy.com/1345/correlation-of-returns-the-reason-why-diversificat.

80 Ibid.

> Spanish philosopher George Santayana said: "Those that do not remember the past are condemned to repeat it." The financial markets have provided investors with enough lessons that there was no reason to make an error such as believing that broad global diversification across equity allocations would protect one from bear markets.[81]

HOLISTIC PORTFOLIO RISK MANAGEMENT APPROACH

It is widely accepted within the financial markets community that there is a need to accept investment risk in order to generate the target returns set out in their investment portfolio strategies. "A natural outworking of this process (that is, investing in assets which are not 'risk free') is that there are likely to be periods where risky investments perform undesirably and poor outcomes occur."[82]

Risk is defined in terms of the standard deviation and volatility of returns, correlation with equity markets, or an overall risk score or measure. But in managing their portfolio risks, financial firms "are typically concerned with avoiding, or at least mitigating the impact of, events that occur infrequently, but which have a large negative impact on portfolio returns. These events are often referred to as 'tail events,' by virtue of the fact that they lie within the left 'tail' of the potential distribution of returns."[83] With the rise of the derivatives market, financial instruments are now available to financial firms that provide some kind of insurance against an array of financial risks.

> However, conventional wisdom and investment theory tells us that the fair price for financial insurance usually exceeds the expected loss that is being protected against. This means that, over the long term, a structural allocation in a portfolio to financial

---

81 Ibid.

82 J. Chee, "Tail Risk Management Strategies," Willis Towers Watson, 2015, https://www.towerswatson.com/en/Insights/IC-Types/Ad-hoc-Point-of-View/2015/10/Tail-risk-management-strategies-oct2015.

83 Ibid.

> insurance will typically result in a drag on returns and, as a result, investor interest in this space tends to be highly cyclical (and often in response to, rather than in advance of, periods of significant market turbulence).
>
> Instead (or as a complement), I propose a holistic approach to portfolio risk management that consists of considering all the risks that affect a portfolio, such as credit, market, liquidity, funding, capital adequacy, compliance, operational, ethical, legal, reputational risks, etc. and their interdependencies, but also tail risk. Such a global view on portfolio risks breaks down the silo approach to portfolio risk management that so often results in duplicated control systems, redundant efforts, and increasing costs.[84]

A holistic portfolio risk management approach also requires closer collaboration and better communication among those involved with managing portfolio risk, thus enhancing information sharing and transparency. It promotes discussion about the different risks and helps people understand the business strategy context of risk, its impact on the business, and how a resolution can benefit all (Mbuya 2010).

Such an approach allows business executives to attain the right information and data and to turn risk awareness into an opportunity to improve business performance. More rating agencies now consider TRM in their rating process, so a sound approach to risk management is beneficial to the enterprise in more ways than one.

Financial organizations that build a holistic portfolio risk and compliance strategy will benefit in two primary ways. First, they are better able to manage and mitigate tail risk and regulatory compliance. This is made possible by collecting and sharing company-wide views on tail risk and compliance. Regulations are always changing, and so is the nature of their enforcement within various jurisdictions.

By effectively monitoring these changes, firms can understand where they may be noncompliant and make the best decisions on where

84 Ibid.

corrective actions are necessary. Similarly, portfolio risks to a firm can best be prioritized when viewed within the context of other risks (such as tail risk) to which it is exposed. Such an enterprise view of risk and compliance enables decision making in the best interests of the firm.

The second key benefit is that institutions can better control the costs of compliance and risk management, ensuring that resources are allocated in the right place. This is particularly true in the case of managing portfolio risk. When a firm optimizes a domain of the business, they must allocate specific funding to each such domain to manage the risk, and the same can be said in regard to portfolios. This would seem prudent, as each area manages a variety of risks, such as a higher risk of fraud in certain types of financial transactions and a lower risk of fraud in others. However, when viewed across the enterprise, these high-risk transactions may be of very low risk and exposure, such that any investment in mitigation could be better deployed elsewhere.

Focus on Resilience, Not on Avoiding Risk

FROM THREAT-CENTRIC TO RESILIENT

Risk is to be managed; it is not something that can entirely be avoided. However, whereas many sought to prevent risk at its source, this view has gradually given way to a more nuanced view that, because risk cannot entirely be avoided, a risk manager's primary efforts should entail building an enterprise robust enough to withstand risks when they do occur. Risk managers need to concentrate efforts on making systems resilient through better internal modeling, designing, and planning. Managers must go from a reactive mind-set to a preventive one.

In other words, we do not manage tail risk merely for tail risk's sake. Instead, we manage tail risk to achieve and optimize the resiliency of the company. That is what risk and controls are all about—increasing the level of confidence in achieving or surpassing objectives to acceptable levels or better. Another obstacle for tail risk practitioners is the language they use. They use the jargon of risk, audit, and controls instead of the language of the business. If one is trying to persuade a manager to embrace new ideas, does one speak to the manager in terms he or she uses or in some strange language that the manager does not understand?

In practice, the whole idea of resilience rests in the fields of engineering, psychiatry, and biology. Resilience is really about the question, "Can a system (be it a firm, a living being, or an organization) resist extreme events, such as a storm, disease, or crisis?" Resilience is also about how an organization bounces back in the face of disruption (Wildavsky 1988).

> Companies should not just evaluate the vulnerabilities of critical systems but also the consequences arising from their disruption. We need to work our way through interdependencies.[85]

Redundancy is seldom explicitly conserved or managed but is just as important as diversity in providing resilience. Focus should be placed on important functions or services with low redundancy, such as those controlled by key actors. In some cases, it may be possible to increase the redundancy associated with these functions. In companies, redundancy consists of apparent inefficiency: idle capacities, unused parts, and money not put to work (Zolli and Healy 2013). The opposite is leverage, which we are taught is good. It is not; debt makes companies—and the economic system—fragile. A highly leveraged company could go under if it neglects a sales forecast, interest rates change, or other risks that occur. If a company is not carrying debt on the books, it can cope better with changes.

> Another myth that hampers resilience is "overspecialization" (Orlov 2013). David Ricardo's theory of comparative advantage recommended that, for optimal efficiency, one country should specialize in making wine, another in manufacturing clothes, and so on. Arguments like this ignore unexpected changes. What will happen if the price of wine collapses? In the 1800s, many cultures in Arizona and New Mexico vanished because they depended on a few crops that could not survive changes in the environment.[86]

---

85 B. Kenealy, "Risk Managers Advised to Focus on Building Resilient Firms," Business Insurance, 2014, http://www.businessinsurance.com/article/20140330/NEWS06/303309970/1235.

86 N. Taleb, "The Six Mistakes Executives Make in Risk Management," *The Harvard Business Review*, 2009, https://hbr.org/2009/10/the-six-mistakes-executives-make-in-risk-management.

Another way to build resilience involves disincentives. The corporate world focuses on incentives and very rarely on disincentives. No one should have a piece of the upside without a share of the downside (or keeping some skin in the game). However, as highlighted by the HBR in "The Six Mistakes Executives Make in Risk Management," "The very nature of compensation adds to risk. If we give someone a bonus without clawback provisions, he or she will have an incentive to hide risk by engaging in transactions that have a high probability of generating small profits and a small probability of blowups."[87]

In the current framework that does not include clawback provisions as they relate to bonuses, senior executives can thus collect variable income for several years, and if blowups eventually do take place, the managers will merely have to apologize but will not have to return past performance–related premiums. This applies to corporations too. "That is why many CEOs become rich, while shareholders stay poor. Society and shareholders should have the legal power to get back the bonuses of those who fail us. That would make the world a better place."[88] Again, no one should have a piece of the upside without a share of the downside. Moreover, we should think twice before offering fat bonuses to those who manage risky establishments, such as nuclear plants and banks. The risks are that they will cut corners to maximize profits; society gives its greatest risk management task to the military, but soldiers do not get bonuses.

In a nutshell, the focus on resilience, as a process, draws attention to the notion of resilient systems. "Resilience is not a state but a dynamic set of conditions, as embodied within a system."[89] A resilient system can be synthetized as follows[90]:

---

87 Ibid.

88 Ibid.

89 K. Harris, "Resilience: A Risk Management Approach," Overseas Development Institute GFDRR, 2012, http://www.gfdrr.org/sites/gfdrr.org/files/ODI.pdf.

90 T. Mitchell, "Resilience: A Risk Management Approach," Overseas Development Institute, 2012, https://www.odi.org/resources/docs/7552.pdf.

√ A high level of diversity, in terms of access to resources, voices included in decision making, and availability of economic opportunities

√ The level of connectivity between institutions and organizations at different entities and the extent to which information, knowledge, evaluation, and learning propagates up and down across these entities

√ The extent to which different forms of knowledge are blended to anticipate and manage processes of change

√ The level of redundancy within a system, meaning some aspects can fail without leading to a whole system collapse

√ The extent to which the system is equal and inclusive of its component parts, not distributing risks in an imbalanced way

√ The degree of social cohesion and human capital, allowing individuals to be supported within embedded social structures

TAIL RISK MANAGEMENT, NOT RISK AVOIDANCE

"The ultimate objective of strong business risk management is not about avoiding risk, but about the ability to take reasonable risk."[91] As a financial firm, you would invest neither in a company that was not taking risk nor in a company that did not have a good risk management function. Without taking risk, there is no opportunity for reward.

> Inadequate risk management practices are almost always a guarantee for a financial wreck.
>
> Unfortunately, all too often this perspective seems to have been lost. Instead, in this sound-bite world the risk management narrative is mostly about eliminating risk to guarantee that financial firms don't lose money. This is neither realistic nor good public policy for an innovation-based economy. The Western

91 M. Ryan, "A Car and Brakes: Risk Management Is Not Risk Avoidance," The BRT Blog, March 27, 2015 http://businessroundtable.org/media/blog/car-and-brakes-risk-management-not-risk-avoidance

> capital markets efficiently take excess capital and allocate it to new ideas and opportunities for growth. Central to this process are strong and pro-business risk management functions within companies.
>
> However, robust risk management is not about complete risk avoidance. Rather, it's about ensuring a company takes reasonable risks along its chosen strategic path, monitors the journey for unexpected dangers and provides that timely steps are taken to minimize losses and to make quick adjustments to keep pace with the competition and meet the needs of consumers.[92]

As stated in Business Roundtable's Principles of Corporate Governance, "It is the responsibility of management, under the oversight of the board, to develop and implement the corporation's strategic plans, and to identify, evaluate and manage the risks inherent in the corporation's strategy."[93] Strong risk management functions integrated into a company's corporate culture promote business success by fostering reasonable risk taking and providing early-detection systems to minimize loss from failures. In any well-run business, a reasonable level of failure must be an option. Without this possibility, the opportunity to take risk in the pursuit of new, innovative, and profitable ideas is lost, and investors, consumers, and the broader economy suffer.

INTEGRATING RISK AND RESILIENCE APPROACHES TO CATASTROPHE MANAGEMENT

Recent natural and human-made catastrophes, such as the Fukushima nuclear power plant, the "flooding caused by Hurricane Katrina, the *Deepwater Horizon* oil spill, the Haiti earthquake, and the mortgage derivatives crisis, have renewed interest in the concept of resilience,

---

92 Ibid.

93 "Principles of Corporate Governance—August 2016," accessed May 4, 2017, https://businessroundtable.org/sites/default/files/Principles-of-Corporate-Governance-2016.pdf.

especially as it relates to complex systems"[94] that are vulnerable to multiple or cascading failures. Although the meaning of resilience is contested in different contexts, in general, resilience is understood to mean the capacity to adapt to changing conditions without catastrophic loss of form or function. In the context of engineering systems, this has sometimes been interpreted as the probability that system conditions might exceed an irrevocable tipping point.

> However, we argue this approach improperly conflates resilience and risk perspectives by expressing resilience exclusively in risk terms. In contrast, we describe resilience as an emergent property of what an engineering system does, rather than a static property the system has. Therefore, resilience cannot be measured at the system scale solely from examination of its component parts. Instead, resilience is better understood as the outcome of a recursive process that includes sensing, anticipating, learning, and adapting. In this approach, resilience analysis can be understood as differentiable from, but complementary to, risk analysis, with important implications for the adaptive management of complex, coupled engineering systems. Management of the 2011 flooding in the Mississippi River Basin has been discussed as an example of the successes and challenges of resilience-based management of complex natural systems that have been extensively altered by engineered structures.[95]

BIGGEST SOURCES OF TAIL RISK EVENTS: INERTIA AND COMPLACENCY

As a risk manager, it is not enough to use ERM to identify, prioritize, treat, and monitor risks. A risk manager is also required to consider the black swans after this process and analyze whether more needs to be done. It

94 J. Park, "Integrating Risk and Resilience Approaches to Catastrophe," Society for Risk Analysis, 2013, https://asu.pure.elsevier.com/en/publications/integrating-risk-and-resilience-ap.

95 Ibid.

is a matter of behaving professionally and being keen to create an added value that will protect, and even help grow, the business. The recent recession, which was caused in part by an erroneous belief that the status quo would continue and the housing market would never decline, is one case in point. Nor is there anything new about the disastrous consequences of complacency; consider the overconfidence of the engineers who built the *Hindenburg* or the misplaced confidence of Spain's King Phillip II "in the ability of his Armada to defeat Queen Elizabeth's British navy. Complacency, after all, is a human characteristic."[96]

This shows that tail events can afflict any culture, not just that of an energy giant or a too-big-to-fail banking institution. It also highlights the importance of organizational culture and a consistent commitment to safety by industry (whether operational or financial safety), from the highest management levels down to the employee. Feeding this inertia is a combination of risk management fatigue toward ever-complex banking regulations with a sense that, as a result of these massive prudential rulings (several thousand pages), all risks ought to be covered.

Senior risk executives seem so overwhelmed by the sheer size of the demands from various stakeholders that they have become confused, perplexed, and even lost on how to improve things from a risk management perspective, given that all their energy has been drained. Risk management (under the instruction of the management board) is inundated with regulations, thereby erasing the desire needed to change, leaving it with no time to look creatively at new risk-management solutions and techniques.

Financial services businesses are likely to be so busy complying with prudential rulings, carrying out internal audit action plans, or conducting regular risk management work that they no longer find time to review the risk management strategies and set up a framework to deal with the risk management of black swans. Alternatively, perhaps the financial activity

96 D. Zavatsky, "Complacency: The Greatest Risk of All," Food Safety News, accessed on April 2, 2017 http://www.foodsafetynews.com/2013/02/complacency-the-greatest-risk-of-all/.

already turns a profit; therefore, businesses do not see the point in reviewing existing risk management plans. Even in the latter case, it is important to realize that, eventually, a TRM strategy will be needed, resulting in a requirement to adapt the ERM framework of the financial institution.

It is important for businesses to fight the urge to remain complacent toward extreme events. They must find the time to reassess their risk management strategies, even if only in a cursory way once a year. Keeping an eye on the marketplace, building an early-warning system, setting up unbiased risk mapping, defining reverse stress testing scenarios, and so on will help businesses know when a revamp of their risk management plans is necessary. But if businesses never conduct an introspective risk management audit, they may be blindsided by the competition or by an extreme risk event carrying such an immense severity in the event of a full-blown exposure that the firm's business model will be wiped out.

Most alternatives are not feasible. Risk avoidance for complacency is impossible unless one replaces every human in the "organization with a robot. To my knowledge, robots do not become complacent. Accepting and monitoring the risk is also not much of a solution. This treatment requires a practitioner to set a baseline monitoring condition,"[97] which, if met, means the risk will be reviewed again for treatment. At best, it means putting off a decision on how to deal with complacency until a later day. At worst, it means the deadly risk event will happen before deciding what to do about it. This was probably one of Lehman Brothers' errors.

"Risk transfer is unlikely to be cost effective; a company that would contract to operate my organization would still need to address complacency risk."[98] Risk hedging does not address the core of the problem in the event of a black swan. Reducing the impact is unfortunately not always an option, because complacency risk often encompasses substantial risks that are game changers outside the control of the organization (such as Lehman Brothers and the global economy or BP and the highly pressurized oil a mile underwater). Reducing the likelihood is the only

97 Ibid.
98 Ibid.

real solution. The likelihood of complacency will decrease if a firm establishes a culture that embraces TRM. At a minimum, such an organization is much more responsive to risks and treatments. It is very unlikely to hear a TRM-savvy CEO say, "I don't care about these risks, as I cannot measure them." Treat complacency risk by creating a high-requirement functioning TRM culture built into the ERM framework.

Mitigating the Impact of Tail Events

FINANCIAL CONTINGENCY PLANNING

A financial contingency plan (FCP) for the worst-case scenario merits inclusion in any strategic planning document. Many financial firms are aware of BCP in relation to operational risk, but oddly enough none exists for financial risk (despite the existence of living wills, regulatory requirements for stress testing, and liquidity adequacy rules); hence, the need for FCP.

FCP is an essential step in building a robust TRM architecture. However, the key for such a framework is to have a financial continuity plan in conjunction with risk mapping, an early-warning system, and (reverse) stress testing tools, because business continuity plans do not focus on financial crises.

It is true there is the concept of a living will, but that regulatory requirement is so cumbersome (several thousand pages) that it is not as practical as standard BCP would be; hence, the need to create a FCP tool. Thus, in practice, what is the distinction between BCP and FCP? While business continuity plans are typically invoked in response to a natural or human-made event, financial continuity plans are invoked when a legal entity or institution has a partial or complete financial failure. Business continuity plans focus on the critical resources required to run the business at a business-process level. Financial continuity plans focus on critical resources at a legal business entity level.

Nominated business staff, who are aware of the functioning of the business and how to recover it, execute business continuity plans. Combined teams that include internal and external staff (regulators, US trustees, and turnaround specialists) working cooperatively with the institution's key executives execute financial continuity plans.

The bottom line is there is no reason to reinvent the wheel, as most of the legwork and effort may have already been completed through the BCP team. Therefore, business continuity team members should be pulled into the FCP process; they have vast knowledge of how all these data fit "together, and much of the necessary data already resides within their business continuity plans and business continuity management databases."[99]

Establishing a partnership across the risk management, finance, legal, and business continuity departments and third-party regulatory advisors should take some of the pain out of developing and maintaining a financial continuity plan and adapting it to the inevitable changes in regulatory requirements. Why not investigate the reuse and repurposing of business continuity data, planning tools, and software to save time and money in preparing the company's financial continuity plan?

Quantification of financial exposure from extreme operational risk exists; however, no such measure is used when extreme financial risks exist. While tail risk for operational business disruption is measured, the effects of a business interruption arising from unexpected, uncertain financial events are not quantified. With such a BCP tool applicable to extreme financial risk, TRM aims to shield the firm from a crisis of confidence.

While financial institutions could adopt best market practices from the manufacturing world, within the array of existing risk management areas, credit, liquidity, capital, and market risk, they would do well to learn from how operational risk is managed.

---

99 J. Beattie, "Did You Know Your Business Continuity Plan Can Help with your Company's Living Will," *Forbes*, 2014, https://www.forbes.com/sites/sungardas/2014/02/24/did-you-know-your-business-continuity-plan-can-help-with-your-companys-living-will/#2b288614406c.

Again, a robust financial continuity plan is a result of an effective stress testing process. Financial firms tend to build mild stress scenarios instead of extreme ones. In addition, firms tend to be optimistic rather than pessimistic about their ability to sustain stress under different scenarios. Obviously, this is because there is a conflict of interest. Business managers involved in the stress testing process will never search and try to uncover potential business weaknesses, as they prefer mild stress tests that would demonstrate the resilience of their business model.

Business managers are optimists by the very nature of their job. This overoptimistic approach can be contagious even for the risk managers involved in the stress testing process. The solution is to assign the task of defining extreme stress scenarios to staff not directly involved in the execution of business activities, such as those in the internal audit, risk management, or even finance departments. In any case, a strong financial continuity plan cannot be put into place without credible extreme risk scenario building and related early-warning tools.

BIG DATA TO MAP AND PREDICT TAIL RISK MANAGEMENT

Just as financial risk models were the mantra for financial institutions in the 2000s, big data seems to be the trend deemed to unleash boundless benefits to its data miners. Indeed, everybody is excited about big data, and organizations all over the world are jumping on the big data bandwagon. The promise of big data is that one could extract lots of information and uncover valuable insight from it. However, while insight is information, not all information provides insight. Practice demonstrates that the amount of valuable insight we can derive from big data is so tiny that we need to collect even more data to increase our chances of gaining insight. In times of worldwide economic crisis, natural disasters, and political turmoil, one often wonders if such events could have been mitigated or avoided altogether with the help of the latest technological developments, such as big data analytics.

It makes sense that financial institutions use predictive analytics by means of big data to improve customer service. Financial institutions collect a ton of information about consumer behavior daily, so why not leverage the benefits of having such vast amounts of data at one's disposal? Using predictive analytics, banks devise more effective ways to manage their relationships with customers, including developing better advertising and marketing campaigns; determining customer buying habits (up-selling and cross-selling initiatives); and creating long-term customer loyalty, retention, screening, and rewards programs.

However, using big data to predict the future from a risk management perspective is a source of difficulty. As previously mentioned, "black swan events are major events that take us by surprise but afterwards yield clear explanations as to why they happened. Examples include the 9/11 attacks, the rise of the Internet, and World War I."[100] They can also apply to business, so there is a temptation to apply big data to predict such black swans before they happen.

This ability to use big data to work across data sets and silos could help us find early clues for hard-to-predict, high-impact black swan events, so we can dig deeper into these clues and assess their validity. When experts investigate catastrophic black swan events, such as airline crashes, financial crises, or terrorist attacks, they often find we failed to anticipate them even when the needed information was present—because the data was spread across different organizations and was never properly brought together.

Unfortunately, black swans, by their very nature, cannot be predicted by analyzing the data. Black swan events do always look eminently predictable in hindsight, yet no one ever predicts them. Equally unfortunate, the more data we throw at the problem, the more impossible it becomes to predict such events. Indeed, the bigger the data set, the harder it becomes to sift through the noise to find the signal, because we are more prone to fixate on incorrect correlations between disparate data sets.

---

100 M. Asay, "Blinded by Big Data: It's the Models, Stupid," ReadWrite, 2013, http://readwrite.com/2013/05/20/blinded-by-big-data/.

In business and economic decision making, data causes severe side effects. Data is now plentiful due to connectivity, and the share of inaccuracy in the data increases as one immerses in it more. A not well-discussed property of data is that it is toxic in large, and even moderate, quantities. The more frequently we look at data, the more noise we "are disproportionally likely to get (rather than the valuable part called the signal)."[101]

The key is that firms should look beyond bigger data toward better models, holding that, historically, it has been about the relative balance and flow between unmodeled and modeled data. The value is not in the data but in the models. Yet, before the Wall Street meltdown, even low-level IT personnel "knew the models were a joke, but our tribal mindset blinded us to the consequences, which may well be the problem."[102] We are human—all too human.

Whether in the models, in the collection of certain kinds of data, or in the interpretation of that data, people bring personal biases to the analysis. We cannot avoid this bias, and the attempt to look for correlation rather than causation in our data solves nothing. In fact, it arguably makes the problem worse because it puts too much confidence in big data.

The trick is to approach big data analytics with caution. It is not that data cannot help us anticipate the future. It can. Just ask the City of Chicago, which has a very successful predictive analytics platform used to anticipate crime and health trends, among other things. There is a reason most enterprises still use big data technologies like Hadoop to solve old problems like ETL, rather than analytics.

We are still early in big data, and enterprises rightly suspect that big data is not some magic pixie dust that immediately yields insight into how much to charge, where to market, and so on. Big data can help, but it is not the answer. It is certainly not the answer to predicting black swan events. To do that, we do not need data; we need hindsight.

---

101 Ibid.

102 Ibid.

Events such as black swans are impossible to predict, so the only approach is to build robust models to mitigate the effects of the negative events and to use the positive events to their fullest potential. Big data analytics is an interesting and useful tool for a researcher dealing with a large amount of data, provided the researcher also has a keen eye that knows how to properly see findings coming from tea-leaf readings.

SUPPLY CHAIN RESILIENCE

A step further down the road of supply chain risk management is the concept of supply chain resilience. Increasing resilience and preventing the cost and revenue impacts of these disruptions affects the entire spectrum of supply chain risks—product, vendor, network, and environmental—as well as demand chain and back-office technology. It requires a new approach—adopting a scenario focus to identify and manage the challenges and opportunities that encompass external events and internal lapses.

As such,

> in today's increasingly dynamic and turbulent world, one where the supply chain plays an increasingly more important role, numerous events occur each day that threaten to disrupt operations and jeopardize the ability to perform effectively and efficiently. These events include natural and man-made disasters such as equipment failures, fires, labor disputes, supplier defaults, political instability, and terrorist attacks.
>
> Each can have devastating effects on a firm. Such disruptions reinforce the insights that not only can supply chain disruptions affect operations; they often result in financial damage well beyond the immediate operational impacts.
>
> One approach to dealing with disruptions is the development of supply chain systems that are resilient. However, this notion of resilience, which is at the heart of so much of our current thinking

about supply chain risk and management, is often not well defined and subject to a great deal of confusion.

While many consultants, researchers, and managers agree on the importance of supply chain resilience, there is less agreement on what it is, how it operates, and how and where to invest to mitigate risk and recover from disruptions—to shape and influence resiliency. This article draws on the expertise of the authors, prior research, anecdotes, and recent events to define and further explore this concept.

Specifically, I propose that resilience happens by design and not by accident. The resilient supply chain requires two critical capacities: the capacity for resistance and the capacity for recovery. The first, resistance, defines the supply chain's ability to delay a disruption and reduce the impact once the disruption occurs. The second, recovery, defines the supply chain's ability to recover from a disruption.[103]

SUPPLY CHAIN RESILIENCE, RISK, AND UNCERTAINTY

The distinctions between supply chain resilience, risk, and uncertainty are often blurred and unclear. Unfortunately, this issue is exacerbated by the fact that some use risk and uncertainty interchangeably, implying that these two concepts are the same. Yet this is not the case. While linked, they are separate and distinct concepts.

Risk exists, so firms have to deal with the possibilities of encountering situations that can adversely affect them. However, not all future events are equally unknown. Past experience offers some insight regarding what events could occur, the probability of occurrence, and the impact.

Firms can predict the likelihood of these events over a set period to help them determine how to potentially react when they occur. Events

---

103 S. Melnyk, "Understanding Supply Chain Resilience," Supply Chain 24/7, Department of Supply Chain Management, Michigan State University, 2011, http://www.supplychain247.com/article/understanding_supply_chain_resilience.

with a greater likelihood and significant potential impact require greater preparation.

In contrast, uncertainty considers unpredictable events. Typically, these are events that have not been previously encountered. Alternatively, they are events where the type of event falls outside of past experience.

Under conditions of uncertainty, such as in the fashion industry, the best approach to building resilience may be to invest in the capacity to recover from an unpredictable disruption. On the other hand, faced with the known risk of a chemical spill, the chemical industry's policy of avoiding such disruptions is more appropriate, especially given the extent of the damage that would otherwise result.

By differentiating between risk and uncertainty, we can uncover an important rule of thumb for resilience: When faced primarily by risk, it makes sense to invest in improving resistance; when dealing with uncertainty, it is more appropriate to invest in improving recovery capabilities.

While there is a great deal of confusion about supply chain resilience, it really comes down to two separate but interrelated elements: resistance and recovery. Further, where your firm chooses to invest in building resilience is really a function of whether you are faced by uncertainty (in which case you invest in recovery) or risk (which justifies the investment in resistance).

Managers can make those investments in supply chain resilience through multiple venues in ways that are appropriate to the risks a firm wants to mitigate and that make sense to the parties involved. The result is that resilience is now becoming a supply chain property that supply chain managers can shape and influence. That happens by design and is no longer a happy accident.

SUSTAINABLE BUSINESS MODEL

There is a need for a crucial shift in regulatory philosophy that looks at systemic risks and the sustainability of business models rather than assuming that all risk can be identified and managed at the level of the individual firm. Flawed business models have led firms to large-scale disasters. Thus, managers should conduct an analysis of the business comfort zones. The concept of comfort zone stems from understanding that each firm has an area business line that is a comfort zone. The comfort zone can be defined as an area of business, product, or service in which the firm has a competitive advantage, core competencies, deep knowledge of risks, and decent control over key risk factors, where all of the above are proved by long, successful business experience in both benign and downturn periods. A comfort zone is an area where a firm is less exposed to risks, including extreme risks. The longer the history of its successful business within the comfort zone, the stronger the ability to moderate its business in different circumstances.

HOW MANAGEMENT PRACTICES, REGULATION, RISK, AND BUSINESS CULTURE NEED TO CHANGE

Contrary to popular belief, the GFC was caused by ineffective management of tail risks by financial institutions—and not by model risks, greed, or globalization. Consequently, the new changes "championed by regulators may not prevent future meltdowns in the financial system unless the fundamental reasons for the crisis are properly addressed."[104] The secret to preventing future financial crises lies in effectively identifying and managing low-probability, high-severity events. Companies must, therefore, inculcate techniques, such as tail risk crisis identification, contingency planning, and tail risk crisis communication, into their regular risk management routines. Obviously, there is no one-size-fits-all solution, but just as firms have business continuity plans from an operational risk perspective, the financial risk aspect should likewise be the object of BCP. A lot could be learned from the existing operational business continuity plan that firms have put in place, and nearly the same disciplined approach should be heralded for financial BCP, namely:

104 Risk Management Events, "Effective Tail Risk Management versus Excessive Protection," https://prmiadc.wordpress.com/themes/governance/effective-tail-risk-management-v.

- building an early-warning system that identifies tail risk, allowing the firm to switch to tail risk alerts;
- developing and implementing a financial continuity plan that should be multileveled;
- ensuring that a solid crisis management framework has been put in place in terms of governance and resources;
- ensuring that data mining and reporting are fast, flexible, arch-encompassing, and detailed enough to allow decision makers to immediately map the risks and take appropriate actions (to that effect, IT will play a key role); and
- communicating with both internal and external stakeholders.

Tail Risk Monitoring

How Tail Risk Monitoring Enables Proactivity

EARLY-WARNING SYSTEM

Generally speaking, I do strongly believe that the approach of waiting for warnings is utterly blemished. The necessary information may never be in your grasp. And even if it were, your "ability to respond rapidly and effectively is far from clear. Rather than treating the symptoms of illness after they start to develop, I believe the better strategy is early immunization: the more resilient the financial system, the less reliance we will have on faulty or nonexistent warnings."[105] And that is what this book has been all about. However, for the sake of completeness, I describe a method that is far from being exhaustive, but that at least will force you to look at the market on an ongoing basis, trying to see if a certain pattern emerges. A defined set of risk indicators and efficient monitoring can lead to significant reduction of risk exposure. Obviously, there has to be a difference between developing an early-warning system for developed countries and doing so for developing countries. However, in this day and age of interconnectedness and globalized economy, contagion effects between both sets of countries do exist.

---

105 S. Cecchetti, "The Mythic Quest for Early Warnings—Money, Banking and Financial," Money and Banking, 2015, http://www.moneyandbanking.com/commentary/2015/4/13/the-mythic-quest-for-early-warnings.

The advantage of building an early-warning system (EWS) is that it compels one to assess the market in an approach that is systematic and data-driven, helping spot the risks that changing global headwinds imply. To that extent, it provides exactly what one needs now: "an approach that removes the need to rely on the ad hoc and slow-moving approach (like the one from the ratings agencies) and the noisy and volatile signals coming from markets. In other words, the 'tail risk' is that by keeping our eyes away from that horizon, we fail to understand and address uncertainties that may lead us to make poor decisions and fail to take necessary actions in running a business."[106] With our eyes away from that horizon, we can lose track of our navigation route and end up where did not intend. Unless we stop talking about the management of tail risk in a defensive way, using the jargon of the tail risk practitioner, and start discussing the optimization of resiliency and sustainability "in a positive way in the language of the business, we are unlikely to succeed."[107] Building more resilient and sustainable business models is the aim.

KEY ELEMENTS OF AN EWS

(1) GOLD

Traditionally, a rising gold price has been a warning sign of trouble ahead as investors buy gold in times of economic turmoil.

The basic proxy for gold is related to the stock price of the South African company called the Randgold Resources Limited.

106 N. Roubini, "China Shows Investors Need a Better Financial Early," MarketWatch, 2015, http://www.marketwatch.com/story/china-shows-investors-need-a-better-financial-early-warning-system-2015-08-27.

107 N. Marks, "Misunderstanding Risk and Controls," Ia Online Home, 2014, https://iaonline.theiia.org/misunderstanding-risk-and-controls.

Previous Close	90.58	Market Cap	8.64B
Open	93.23	Beta	-0.11
Bid	90.90 x 100	PE Ratio (TTM)	35.14
Ask	91.50 x 100	EPS (TTM)	2.61
Day's Range	91.03 - 94.15	Earnings Date	N/A
52 Week Range	67.54 - 126.55	Dividend & Yield	1.00 (1.06%)
Volume	1,044,966	Ex-Dividend Date	N/A
Avg. Volume	988,398	1y Target Est	101.93

Trade prices are not sourced from all markets

From Yahoo Finance.[108]

(2) VIX

This chart shows rolling realized correlations for the top stocks of the S&P 500 compared to the VIX.

The "VIX is a trademarked ticker symbol for the CBOE Volatility Index, a popular measure of the implied volatility of S&P 500 index options; the VIX is calculated by the Chicago Board Options Exchange (CBOE)."[109]

> A markets rule of thumb is that in times of crises or when macro currents are ruling the state of play vs individual company and sector fundamentals, correlations go towards 1 (e.g. look back to 2008 when correlations converged big time). So it makes a degree

108 Yahoo Finance Randgold Resources Limited, accessed January 1, 2017, https://finance.yahoo.com/quote/GOLD.

109 "VIX chart and CBOE Volatility Index," TradingView, https://www.tradingview.com/chart/VIX/?exg=INDEX.

of sense that low correlations go with low volatility and high correlations go with high volatility. Interestingly, from the very limited history in that chart it looks like periods of low correlations tend to precede rises in the VIX.[110]

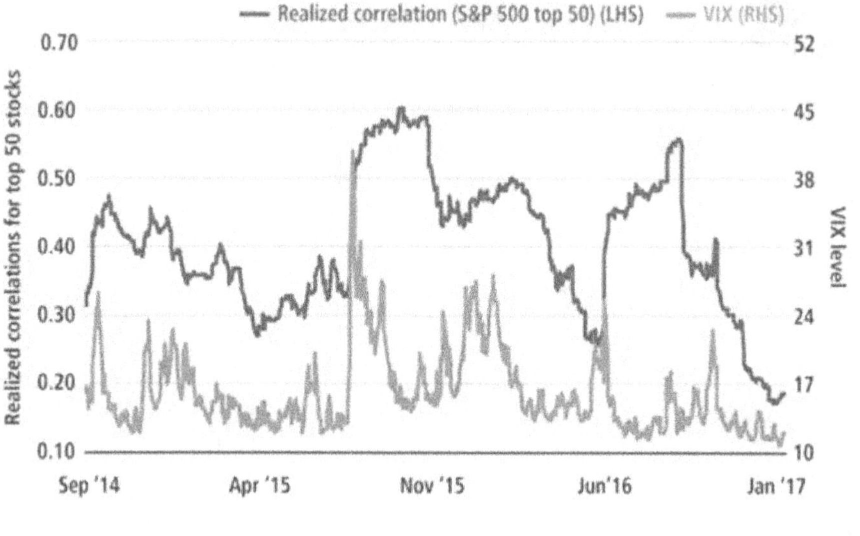

From Bloomberg.[111]

(3) CRUDE OIL PRICE

Typically, increasing oil prices suggest higher risks, while lowering energy prices indicate a rebound in confidence.

110 "Weekly S&P 500 #ChartStorm," accessed February 12, 2017, http://www.minyanville.com/business-news/markets/articles/2524SPX-2524SPY/2/12/2.

111 Bloomberg VIX Quote and S&P 500, accessed January 31, 2017, https://www.bloomberg.com/quote/VIX:IND; Bloomberg VIX Quote and S&P 500, accessed January 31, 2017.

From Y-Chart.[112]

(4) THE YIELD CURVE

In general, the greater the difference between the yield on the two-year and the yield on the ten-year US Treasury notes, the more growth the market is pricing into the economy. This yield difference is sometimes called the yield curve because of how steep or flat it looks when the yield for each maturity is plotted on a chart.

112 "Y-Chart, WTI Crude Oil Spot Price," accessed January 31, 2017, https://ycharts.com/indicators/crude_oil_spot_price.

Treasury Yield Curve

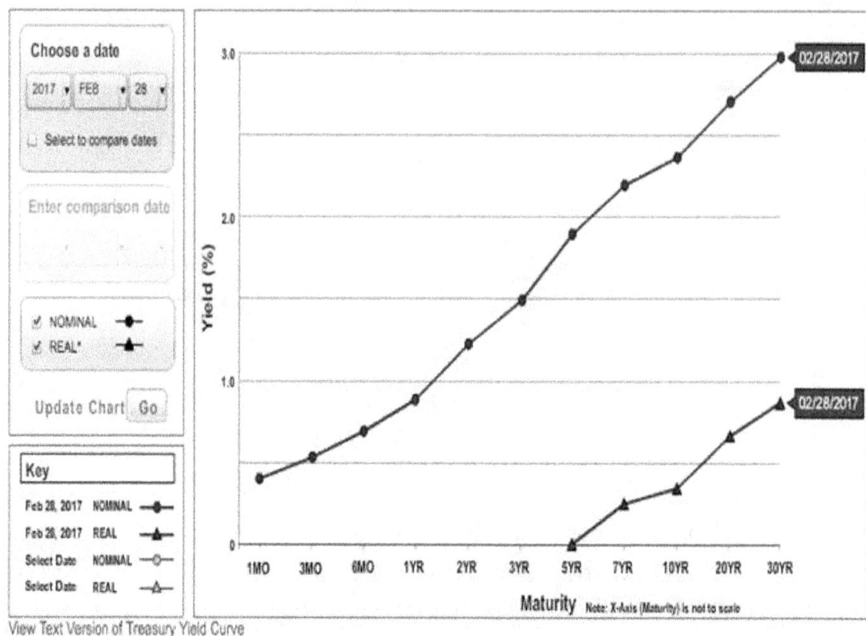

* Data for real maturities may not be available for all dates for which nominal maturity data is available.

From Treasury.gov.[113]

113 "Treasury—Daily Treasury Yield Curve Rates," accessed February 28, 2017, https://www.treasury.gov/resource-center/data-chart-center/interest-rates/Pages/TextView.aspx?data=yield.

(5) EARNINGS OUTLOOK

An earnings estimate is an analyst's estimate for a company's future quarterly or annual earnings. Future-earnings estimates are arguably the most important input when attempting to value a firm.

"Guidance is information a company provides as an indication or estimate of its future earnings. It is an 'expected results' issue from a company to shareholders and market watchers as to how it envisions a future period turning out."[114]

The graph below shows to what level the S&P 500 will rise by the end of 2017 according to the different investment banks on Wall Street:

2017 Wall Street Year-End S&P 500 Targets

Firm	2017 Year-End Target at Start of Year	% From Current S&P 500 Level
RBC	2,500	10.13
Oppenheimer	2,450	7.93
Citigroup	2,425	6.83
Barclays	2,400	5.73
Deutsche Bank	2,400	5.73
JP Morgan	2,400	5.73
Bank of Montreal	2,350	3.52
Scotiabank	2,350	3.52
Weeden	2,350	3.52
Canaccord	2,340	3.08
Jefferies	2,325	2.42
Bank of America	2,300	1.32
Credit Suisse	2,300	1.32
Goldman Sachs	2,300	1.32
Stifel Nicolaus	2,300	1.32
UBS	2,300	1.32
Average	2,362	4.05

From Bespoke Investment Group.[115]

114 "Guidance Definition," Investopedia, http://www.investopedia.com/terms/g/guidance.asp.

115 "Wall Street Strategists Bearish on 2017?," Bespoke Investment Group, last modified December 26, 2016, https://www.bespokepremium.com/think-big-blog/wall-street-strategists-bearish-on-2017/.

(6) STIMULUS CENTRAL BANK

An accommodative monetary policy indicates that the central bank is injecting vast sums of liquidity, thereby keeping rates low with the hope that it will help boost the local economy.

However, when the accommodative policy lasts too long, it might show that the fundamentals of the economy are really weak, structurally speaking.

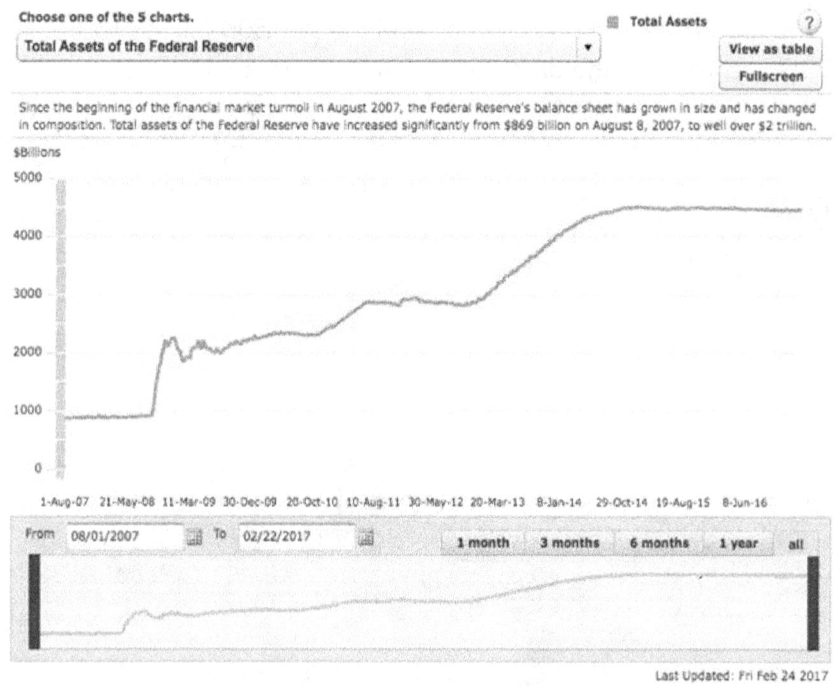

From Federal Reserve Bank of Saint Louis.[116]

116 "Federal Reserve Bank of St Louis," accessed February 22, 2017, https://fred.stlouisfed.org/series/WALCL.

(7) THREE-MONTH EURIBOR AND LIBOR RATES

LIBOR (London Interbank Offered Rate) and Euribor (Euro Interbank Offered Rate) used to be good indicators; however, the banking manipulation scandal has cast a lot of doubts about the predicting power of these two rates.

The Euribor and LIBOR are the reference rates "at which large banks indicate that they can borrow short-term wholesale funds from one another on an unsecured basis in the interbank market,"[117] and also to index billions of dollars of bonds and loans.

> Beginning in 2007, regulators and market observers noted that LIBOR/Euribor had failed to behave in line with expectations given other market prices and rates.
>
> Investigations by U.S. and foreign regulators have uncovered explicit manipulation by banks to influence rate fixings with the intent of projecting financial soundness during the crisis and benefiting proprietary trading positions.[118]

Three-month Euribor interest rate

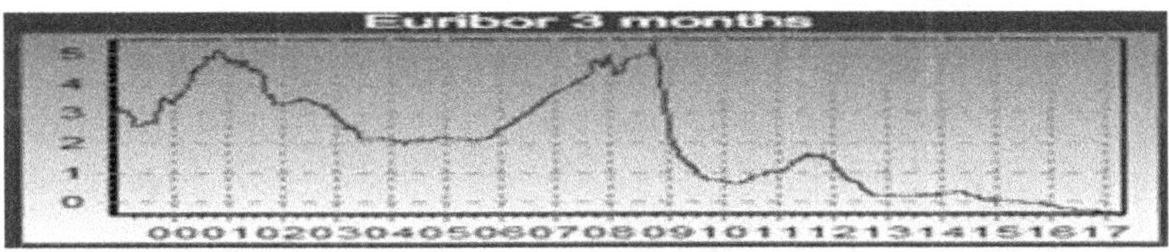

From Euribor-rates.[119]

117 "LIBOR: Origins, Economics, Crisis, Scandal, and Reform," https://www.newyorkfed.org/medialibrary/media/research/staff_reports/sr667.pdf.

118 Ibid.

119 "Three-Month Euribor Interest Rate," Euribor-rates.eu, accessed January 31, 2017, http://euribor-rates.eu/euribor-charts.asp.

Three-month CHF LIBOR interest rate

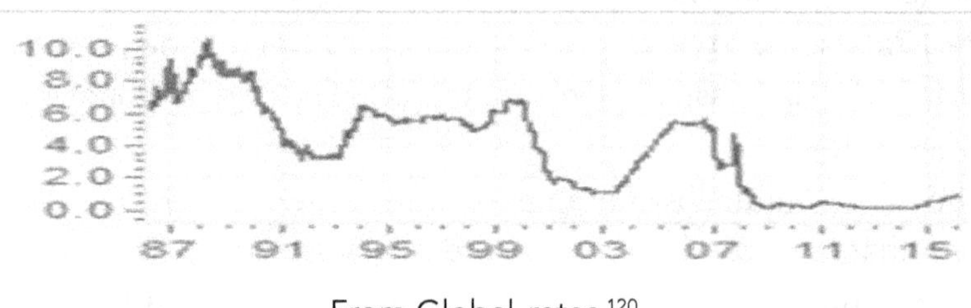

From Global-rates.[120]

(8) TWO-YEAR SWAP SPREAD

A swap spread is the difference between the rate on a two-year interest-rate swap and the US Treasury. "Swap rates serve as benchmarks for investors in many types of debt often purchased with borrowed money, including mortgage-backed securities and auto-loan securities. Narrower swap spreads can push borrowing costs lower even if Treasury yields are steady."[121]

In other words,

> because banks and other financial institutions are the folks trading swaps, the tightening spreads indicate the health of the banking sector, and depth of liquidity in the market.
>
> Swap spreads have a record—albeit not a very long record—of anticipating changes in the health of the economy. They rose in advance of the past three recessions, and fell in advance of the past three recoveries. Currently, swap spreads remain unusually low, a sign that financial markets enjoy plenty of liquidity and there is little if any fear that conditions in the financial markets or the economy will deteriorate meaningfully in the next two years.[122]

---

120 "Three-Month CHF LIBOR Interest Rate," Global-rates.com, accessed January 31, 2017, http://global-rates.com/interest-rates/libor/swiss-franc/chf-libor-interest-rate-3-months.aspx.

121 L. C. McCormick, "U.S. 2-Year Swap Spread Reaches Widest in a Year as Stocks," Bloomberg, 2014, https://www.bloomberg.com/news/articles/2014-08-08/u-s-2-year-swap-spread-reaches-widest-in-a-year-as-stocks-drop.

122 B.Eisen,"SoWhatDoesaShrinkingSwapSpreadMeanAnyway?,"MarketWatch,2013, http://blogs.marketwatch.com/thetell/2013/12/18/so-what-does-a-shrinking-swap-sp.

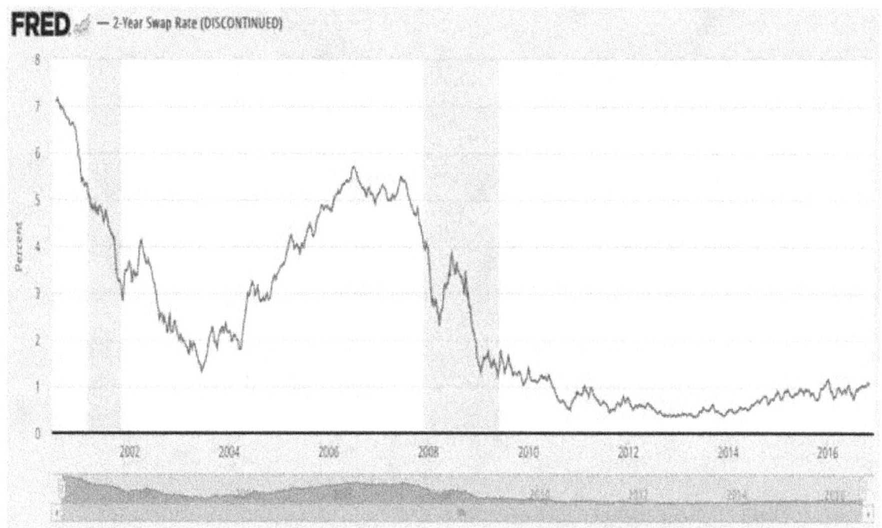

From Federal Reserve Bank of Saint Louis.[123]

(9) TED SPREAD

The TED spread is a classic systemic risk indicator. It is the difference between the interest rates on interbank loans and on short-term US government debt ("T-bills"). TED is an acronym formed from T-Bill and ED, the ticker symbol for the Eurodollar futures contract.

The TED spread is an indicator of perceived credit risk in the general economy because T-bills are considered risk-free, "while LIBOR reflects the credit risk of lending to commercial banks.

"An increase in the TED spread is a sign that lenders believe the risk of default on interbank loans (also known as counterparty risk) is increasing. Interbank lenders, therefore, demand a higher rate of interest or accept lower returns on safe investments, such as T-bills. When the risk of bank defaults"[124] is decreasing, the TED spread decreases.

123 "Two-Year Swap Rate," Federal Reserve Bank of St Louis, accessed January 31, 2017, https://alfred.stlouisfed.org/series?seid=WSWP2.

124 *Wikipedia*, s.v. "TED spread," https://en.wikipedia.org/wiki/TED_spread.

From MacroTrends.[125]

(10) CREDIT SPREAD BETWEEN BIG BANKS AND INDUSTRIALS

"Markit iTraxx indices allow investors to express their bullish or bearish sentiments on credit as an asset class and portfolio managers to manage their credit exposures actively."[126]

Markit iTraxx are the standard European and Asian tradable credit default swap family of indices. The rules-based Markit iTraxx indices comprise "the most liquid names in the European and Asian markets. The selection methodology ensures that the indices are replicable and represent the most liquid, traded part of the market."[127]

The graph below can be read as follows:

- As of March 31, 2017, the iTraxx Europe Senior Financial (consisting of twenty-five financial entities from the Markit iTraxx Europe index referencing senior debt) was at 74.7 bps.

125 "TED Spread," MacroTrends, accessed January 31, 2017, http://www.macrotrends.net/1447/ted-spread-historical-chart.

126 "iTraxx," Markit, http://www.markit.com/product/ITraxx.

127 "Appendix," Markit Credit and Loan Indices, https://www.safaribooksonline.com/library/view/credit-derivatives-trading/978047.

- The benchmark Markit iTraxx Europe index comprises 125 equally weighted European names, and as of end March 2017, it was at 58.6 bps.

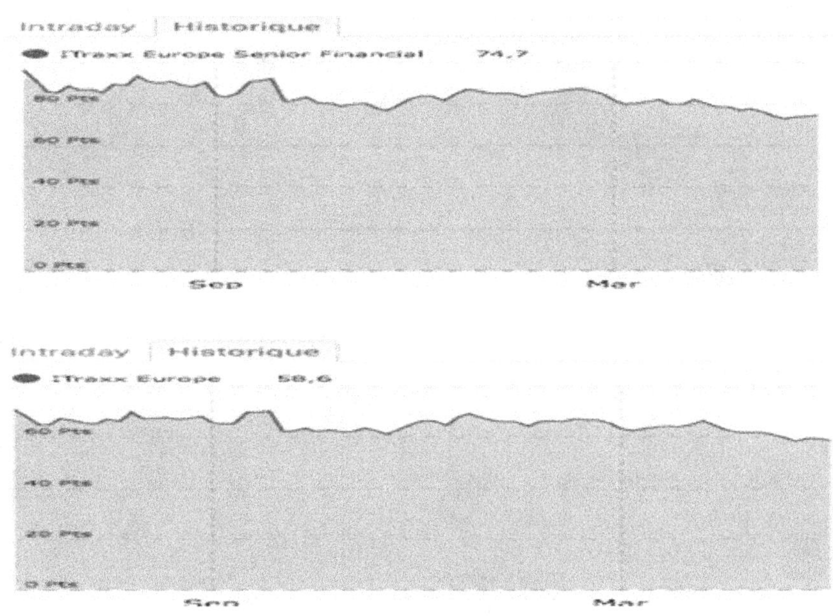

From Boursorama.[128]

(11) CDS SPREAD

"Credit Default Swap (CDS) is a financial swap agreement that the seller of the CDS will compensate the buyer (usually the creditor of the reference loan) in the event of a loan default (by the debtor) or other credit event. This is to say that the seller of the CDS insures the buyer against some reference loan defaulting.

"The buyer of the CDS makes a series of payments (the CDS 'fee' or 'spread') to the seller and, in exchange, receives a payoff if the loan defaults."[129] It was invented by Blythe Masters from JP Morgan in 1994.

128 "iTraxxEuropeSeniorFinancial," Boursorama, accessed March 31, 2017, http://www.boursorama.com/bourse/taux/cds-ITraxx_Europe_Senior_Financial-3xItraxxESF.

129 "What Is Credit Default Swaps," DeZyre, https://www.dezyre.com/questions/3494/what-is-credit-default-swaps.

For example, the international commercial banks below show the following CDS spreads (as of March 31, 2017):

Credit Default Swaps (CDS)	
Unternehmen	Credit Default Swaps
Banco Santander	98,91
Bank of America	63,47
BARCLAYS Bank	78,14
Bayerische Landesbank	---
BHF-Bank[1)]	---
BNP Paribas	89,22
Bundesrepublik Deutschland	17,85
Citigroup[2)]	62,94
Commerzbank	110,76
Crédit Agricole	83,26
Credit Suisse	103,30
Deka	---
Deutsche Bank	126,74
DZ BANK[3)]	---
EFG International AG	---
Erste Group Bank	112,15
Eurobank Ergasias S.A.	1.212,60
Goldman Sachs	82,93
HSBC Trinkaus[4)]	63,89
HSH Nordbank	185,02
HypoVereinsbank/UniCredit Bank AG	90,71
ING-Bank	60,51
J.P. Morgan	55,80
LBBW	47,00
Landesbank Berlin	---
Landesbank Hessen-Thueringen	73,20
Lloyds Banking Group plc	65,47
Macquarie Bank Ltd.	76,59
Morgan Stanley	80,62
Morgan Stanley & Co. International PLC	---
NATIXIS	81,15
Nomura Bank International	46,56
Norddeutsche Landesbank	---
Österreichische Volksbanken	---
Rabobank	52,70
Raiffeisen Centrobank	---
RBS N.V. (ehemals ABN AMRO Bank N.V.)	86,04
Royal Bank of Scotland plc	93,50
Sal. Oppenheim [5)]	---
SEB	39,39
Société Générale	89,92
UBS Investment Bank	55,04
Vontobel [6)]	---
WGZ BANK[7)]	---

From Boerse.[130]

(12) CORRELATION BETWEEN STOCKS AND OIL PRICES

"It is popular to correlate changes in major factor prices, such as oil, and the performance of major stock market indexes. Conventional wisdom holds that an increase in oil prices will raise input costs for most businesses and force consumers to spend more money on gasoline, thereby

130 "CDS Spreads," Boerse.de, accessed March 31, 2017, http://www.boerse.de/derivate/credit-spreads/.

reducing the corporate earnings of other businesses. The opposite should be true when oil prices fall."[131]

However, there is very little correlation between the oil prices and the stock markets (even though sometimes they have been correlated, as in early 2016). This does not necessarily prove that the price of oil has a very limited impact on stock market prices. It does suggest, however, that no one can really predict the way stocks react to changing oil prices.

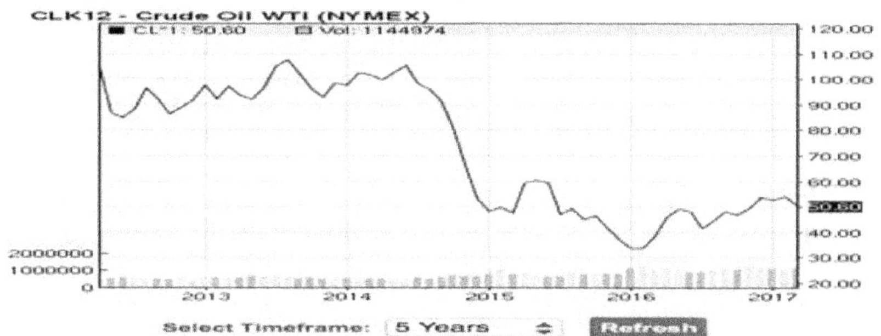

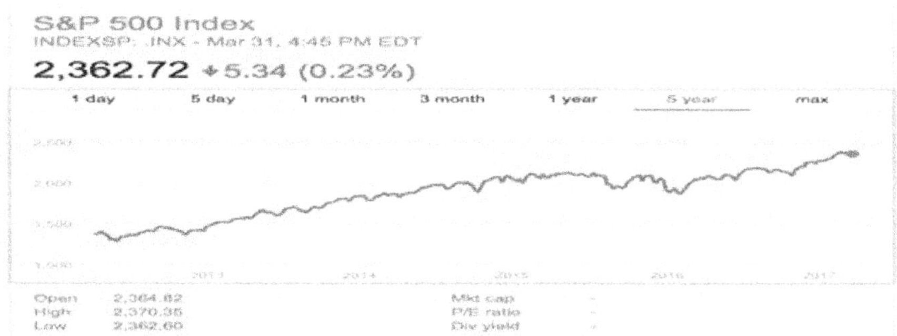

From Nasdaq and Yahoo Finance.[132]

131 How Does the Price of Oil Affect the Stock Market," Investopedia, http://www.investopedia.com/ask/answers/030415/how-does-price-oil-affect-stock-m.

132 "Nymex Crude Oil," Nasdaq, accessed March 31, 2017, http://www.nasdaq.com/markets/crude-oil.aspx; "S&P 500 Index," Yahoo Finance, accessed March 31, 2017, https://au.finance.yahoo.com/quote/%5EGSPC?ltr=1.

(13) PERCENT OF STOCKS ABOVE THEIR FIFTY-DAY MOVING AVERAGE

"The percentage above a moving average indicator can be a great tool to monitor the 'health' of a market and see in greater context how stocks are performing as a whole."[133]

You can use the percentage of stocks above a moving average when the indicator for the indices breaks below a certain level. I often watch for a break of 30 percent. This means that less than 30 percent of stocks are above their fifty-day moving average.

As highlighted in the graph below, as of April 2, 2017, 60 percent of the S&P 500 stocks were trading above their fifty-day moving average.

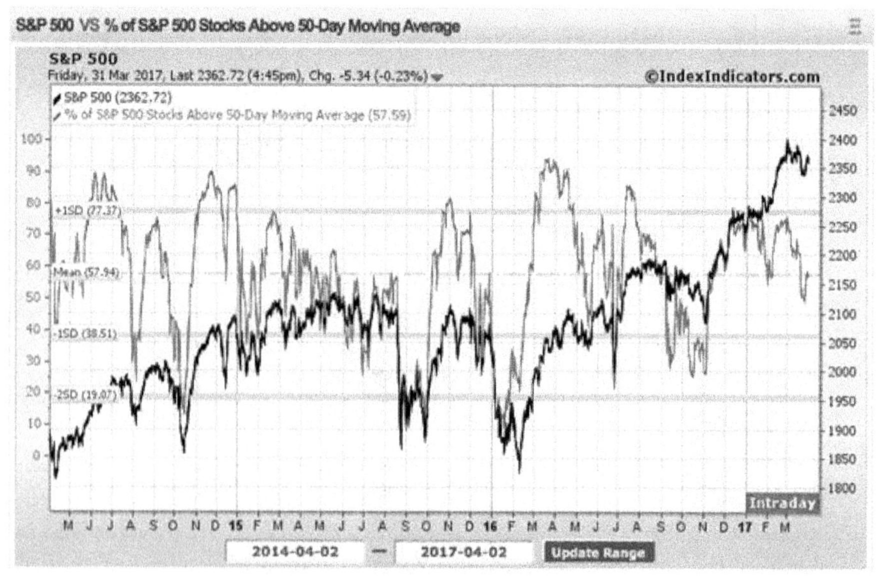

From IndexIndicators.com.[134]

133 "Percentage of Stocks above Their Moving Average," http://www.traderplanet.com/articles/view/164822-percentage-of-stocks-above-thei.

134 "S&P 500 vs% S&P 500 Stocks Above 50-day Moving Average," IndexIndicators.com, accessed April 2, 2017, http://www.indexindicators.com/charts/sp500-vs-sp500-stocks-above-50d-sma-params-3y-x-x-x.

(14) CHICAGO BOARD OPTIONS EXCHANGE PUT–CALL RATIO

The put–call ratio is a gauge that shows the volumes of put options relative to the volume of call options. Put options are essentially used to protect against market weakness or gamble on a decline, whereas call options are used to shield against market strength or gamble on advance.

When a put–call ratio is above 1, it means that the put volume exceeds call volume, while below 1 when call volume exceeds put volume. Typically, this indicator is used to gauge market sentiment. Sentiment is deemed excessively bearish when the put–call ratio is trading at relatively high levels, and excessively bullish when at relatively low levels.[135]

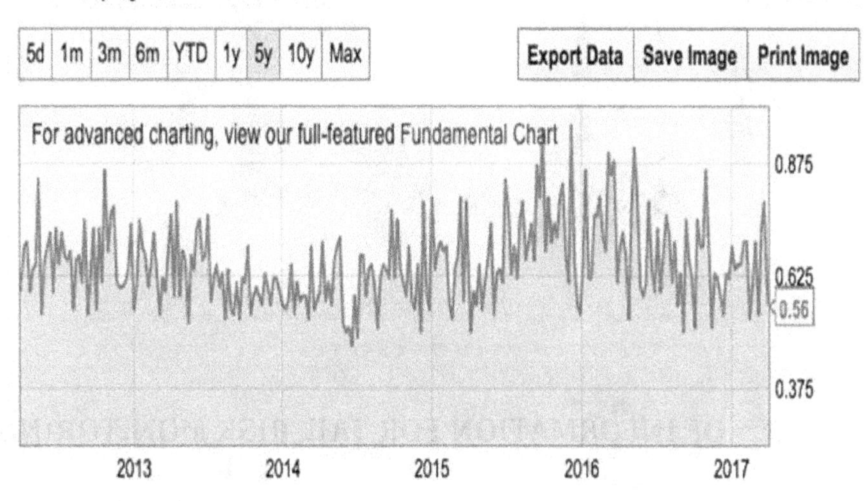

From Y-Charts.[136]

135 "Put/Call Ratio," StockCharts.com, http://www.stockcharts.com/school/doku.php?id=chart_school:technical_indicators.

136 "CBOE Equity Put/Call Ratio," Ycharts.com, accessed April 2, 2017, https://ycharts.com/indicators/cboe_equity_put_call_ratio.

(15) CORPORATE DEFAULT RATE

A popular measure of loan defaults is the default rate, and both Moody's and Standard & Poor's keep track of these indicators.

Typically, "declining loan defaults signal a recovering economy. This one is more of a lagging indicator, as it's during the recovery phase of the economy that economic activity increases, leading to increases in money flows and leaving people in a better position to service their loan obligations. In a recessionary economy, more and more people default on their loan obligations, as inflationary pressures squeeze disposable income."[137]

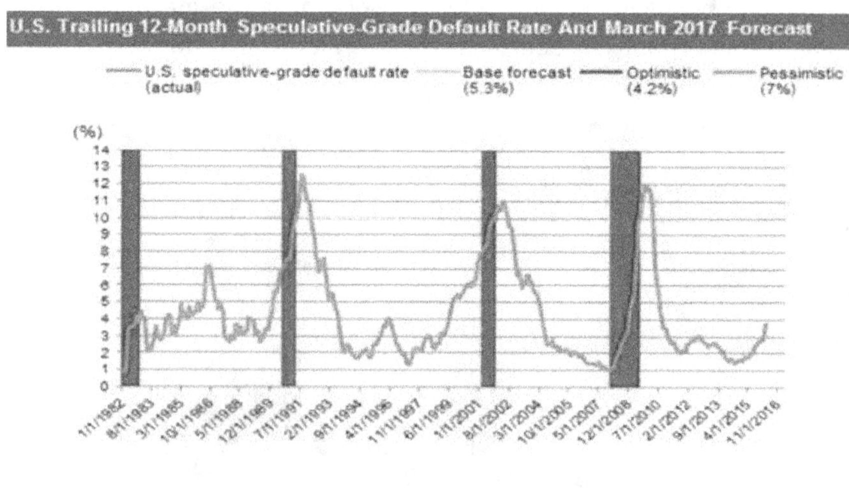

Note: Shaded areas are periods of recession as defined by the National Bureau of Economic Research. Sources: S&P Global Fixed Income Research and S&P Global's

SOURCES OF INFORMATION FOR TAIL RISK MONITORING PROCESS

The purpose of risk management is to identify potential problems before they occur so that risk-handling activities may be planned and invoked as needed across the life of the product or project to mitigate

137 S. Jain, "Why Leading Indicators and the Default Rate Help Predict," Yahoo Finance, 2014, http://finance.yahoo.com/news/why-leading-indicators-default-rate-192404433.html.

adverse effects on achieving objectives. "Risk management is a continuous, forward-looking process that is an important part of business and technical management processes. Risk management should address issues that could endanger achievement of critical objectives. A continuous risk management approach is applied to effectively anticipate and mitigate the risks" that have a critical impact on the project.[138] ERM includes early and aggressive risk identification through the collaboration and involvement of relevant stakeholders. Strong leadership across all relevant stakeholders is needed to establish an environment for the free and open disclosure and discussion of risk.

Businesses should demonstrate that there is a process to determine risk sources and categories. Identification of risk sources provides a basis for systematically examining changing situations over time to uncover circumstances that affect "the ability of the project to meet its objectives. Risk sources are both internal and external to the project. As the project progresses, additional sources of risk may be identified. Establishing categories for risks provides a mechanism for collecting and organizing risks as well as ensuring appropriate scrutiny and management attention for those risks that can have more serious consequences on meeting project objectives. Typical work products would include 1) risk source lists (external and internal) and 2) risk categories lists."[139]

Businesses should have a "process to define the parameters used to analyze and categorize risks and the parameters used to control the risk management effort. Parameters for evaluating, categorizing, and prioritizing risks typically include risk likelihood (i.e., the probability of risk occurrence), risk consequence (i.e., the impact and severity of risk occurrence), and thresholds to trigger management activities. Risk parameters are used to provide common and consistent criteria for comparing the various risks to be managed. Without these parameters, it would be very difficult to gauge the severity of the unwanted change caused by the risk

138 "Risk Process Guidelines," The Mitre Corporation accessed April 2, 2017 http://www2.mitre.org/work/sepo/toolkits/risk/compliance/files/RiskProcessGuidelines.doc.
139 Ibid.

and to prioritize the necessary actions required for risk mitigation planning. Typical work products would include 1) risk evaluation, categorization, and prioritization criteria and 2) risk management requirements (e.g., control and approval levels, reassessment intervals)."[140]

In most organizations, the existing approach has involved dividing risk into three main categories: financial, operational, and strategic. Companies have generally done a good job of focusing on the first two of these risks: financial and operational. However, they have often been less successful at linking these risk categories together or understanding the interdependencies between them. Moreover, many businesses have focused much less attention on strategic risk, largely because they regard risk and strategy as separate from each other, rather than seeing risk taking as a key part of value creation in any business. That is where early warnings, red flags, or gray swans come into play.

A common mistake in risk management is to refuse to face the facts and be unwilling to prepare for upcoming events. Senior executives are falling too easily into the sunk-cost fallacy trap, alleging that because the stakes are so high (i.e., because firms are emotionally invested in whatever money, time, or other resource they have committed in the past), retreating and preparing for the worst would be unacceptable. Indeed, many senior risk management executives opt to ignore signs of danger instead of trying to maximize recovery values in case of loss scenarios.

One of the most compelling examples illustrating the failure to react to red flags is the recent GFC. Indeed, notwithstanding a hard-to-quell, enduring myth alleging that everybody missed the early-warning signals, there were a lot of signs of an upcoming crisis, but no one paid real attention to them.

Therefore, when going through the financial statements and other related firm reports, risk management should ensure that the firm provides adequate and timely financial and performance information that can answer questions such as the following:

140 Ibid.

- Is the bank's strategic plan realistic for its circumstances?
- Is management meeting the goals established in the planning process and, if not, why?
- Is the level of earnings consistent or erratic?
- Do earnings result from the implementation of planned bank strategies or from transactions that, while increasing short-term earnings, raise longer-term risk?
- Do audit programs test internal controls to identify inaccurate, incomplete, or unauthorized transactions; deficiencies in the safeguarding of assets; unreliable financial and regulatory reporting; violations of law and regulations; and deviations from the institution's policies and procedures?
- Are policies and procedures in place to safeguard against conflicts of interest, insider fraud and abuses, and affiliate abuse?
- Is the bank giving due consideration to changes in external conditions?
- Is the bank compensated adequately for the risks it is taking in its various product lines and activities?
- Does the bank have sufficient capital to support its risk profile and business strategies?
- Are financial reports and statements accurate, or do they reflect an incomplete evaluation of the bank's financial condition?
- Are the bank's goals and plans consistent with the directors' tolerance for risk?

COLLABORATIVE MANAGEMENT BETWEEN RISK, FINANCE, AND BUSINESS DEVELOPMENT MANAGERS

Risk management has many stakeholders, two of them being finance and front office.

In addition, as a result of the tightening regulatory environment, the traditional model to manage regulatory risks becomes unviable; the risk function will need to build even more robust stakeholder-management capabilities.

Finance has traditionally been involved in the management of financial risks through the use of derivatives, insurance, and other financial instruments, and as such finance is already familiar with many terms and concepts related to risk. Additionally, from an accounting perspective, finance is already reporting risk exposures in relation to assets on the balance sheet of the financial firm.

With that in mind, the risk management department within the financial firm needs to work more closely with the finance department, as they use many of the same tools and extract data from the same databases (risk exposures, economic capital, probability of default, loss given default, expected loss, exposure at default, etc.). The key is to have the same understanding about risk metrics and risk taxonomy, such as risk exposures, provisions, exposure at default, expected loss, and numerous other risk reporting data.

In addition, the risk function needs to play a vital role in collaborating with other functions, such as with the business with the aim to reduce risk—by working more closely with the front office to integrate and automate the correct behaviors and to eliminate human interventions.

Let's keep in mind that in the spirit of the "three lines of defense" approach, the front office owns the risks. Line management is indeed "responsible for identifying and managing risks directly (design and operation of controls). This group has to regard risk management as a crucial element of their everyday jobs."[141] As such, the risk function's tasks will be to ensure that compliance considerations are always top of mind and not addressed perfunctorily by businesses after they have formulated their strategies or designed a new product.

Generally speaking, given the increased demands from regulators and other stakeholders alike, promoting the close collaboration between finance and risk on the one hand and business and risk on the other hand

---

141 J. Feliciano, "The Risk Management of Product Design," Intercompany Long Term Care Insurance, 2017, http://iltciconf.org/index_htm_files/44-Risk%20Mgmt%20session.pdf.

will improve the capability by which the firm will be able to produce on demand ad hoc reports. To that end, risk, business, and finance need to use management information systems that are very similar so that data exchanges between risk, business, and finance can be greatly facilitated.

Takeaway Messages

How Tail Risk Management Can Turn a Headwind into a Tailwind

One of the most effective ways to manage tail risk in a global enterprise is to transform the culture into one of risk awareness, identification, analysis, and mitigation. Tail risk hedging strategies can be a temporary solution, but do not provide a structural shield for protecting portfolios and business models from downside risks. Since 2008, the desire to avoid significant losses has, more than ever, been at the front of senior executives' minds. The approach to managing downside risk or tail risk has been restricted in a primeval way to tail risk hedging strategies. However, as I already mentioned, these strategies are costly and not necessarily efficient. In any case, while tail risk hedging strategies necessarily differ for every firm, a sustained TRM can be applied across all types of firms (see my proposal for a three-pronged approach below).

Since the GFC in 2008, "the demand for strategies that protect against significant negative returns has increased substantially. It is partly the fear that we are in a market environment unfamiliar to most market participants with limited central bank policy options and with uncertain outcomes that have led to this interest."[142] Meanwhile, yields on "safe-haven" government bonds have fallen so low that there is no obvious

---

142 A. Forest, "Effective Downside Risk Management," Schroders Global, 2016, http://www.schroders.com/en/sysglobalassets/digital/expert-magazine/pdfs/sro_expert-19_3_2016_en.pdf.

diversifying asset. Traditional balanced portfolios have better diversified over time through the addition of new asset classes, but increased globalization and the consequent interdependence of asset classes have led to an increase in their correlation in times of crisis.

Institutional investors and other stakeholders look for new ways to "limit risks as they face greater pressure from stakeholders to be better protected in the event of a repeat of the 2008 crisis. This is evidenced by an exponential increase in the demand for volatility-based instruments, such as options and volatility futures,"[143] but as already mentioned, hedging instruments are merely a temporary solution to long-term problems. As an alternative to resorting to (quantitative) hedging instruments, I propose a three-pronged approach to TRM:

1. Be cognizant of the environment in which you are operating (through risk mapping and early-warning systems).
2. Have a clear understanding of where your most vulnerable link in your company is (through scenario analysis, reverse stress testing, risk strategy and appetite, and supply chain risk management).
3. Know what actions can be taken to prevent your company from falling to its knees (through FCP, supply chain resilience, and building a sustainable business model).

TOOLKIT: TAIL RISK DEFENSE

TRM is not

- traditional risk management,
- ERM,
- capital management,
- threat-centric,
- Basel III (Dodd-Frank, CRDIV, etc.),
- hedging strategies,
- prediction tools,

143 Ibid.

- based on probability theory, or
- designed to protect revenue opportunities.

TRM is

- just-in-case risk management,
- part of strategic risk management,
- building resiliency,
- helping build a sustainable model,
- preservation of the firm's survivability,
- relating to unknown scenarios,
- incentivizing redundancy, and
- uncertainty management.

FAT-TAIL THINKING

A "fat tail" is industry shorthand for a fat-tailed distribution, a probability distribution that exhibits extremely large "skewness," meaning there are a number, sometimes a large number, of data that lie outside a normal distribution pattern. Tails can be skewed negatively (very low prices to the left of normal) or positively (very high prices to the right).

Risk managers are usually aware that fat tails exist, and they are familiar with the power laws (a power law is a relationship between two quantities such that one is proportional to a fixed power of the other) that reveal themselves through statistical modeling. However, having no other rational way to model the effects of tails, to say nothing of hedging against them, they ignore them when modeling risks and hedge performance.

Fat-tail risks should be understood as a type of risk that interacts with other sources of risk in a business or investment portfolio. A negative event will tend to increase the risk premium and alter the direction of (business) asset prices. One that depresses economic growth and changes the course of inflation is likely to have a sustained effect. Meanwhile, the direction of the impact will depend on the asset in question, and the magnitude will depend on the severity and resolution of the incident.

The key to assessing the business implications of fat-tail risks lies in understanding how they affect the main drivers of a company's capital returns. Fortunately, the same variables that are relevant in any generic investment context are relevant here. Investors and entrepreneurs need to remain aware of the critical and ever-changing landscape, understand how these shocks can affect various assets within a portfolio, and regard geopolitics as central to the investment decision, rather than simply as an afterthought.

SENIOR EXECUTIVES STILL DO NOT GET IT

Senior leadership typically does not get it, as financial firms, despite recent regulatory rules (Dodd-Frank, EMIR, and Basel III), largely continue to operate only in the context of known risks that can be priced. Uncertainty management needs to focus beyond the pricing of known risk, as actual results are also determined by how unknown events and market conditions can unfold. In extreme scenarios, unexpected losses can exceed the capital and thus threaten the survival of the institution. Therefore, the objective of TRM must be to leverage resources to mitigate and absorb unexpected losses in such a way that the capital (firm) is always protected and preserved.

Enthralled by new revenue opportunities, over the last twenty-five years, the industry has been focusing on what quantitative analysis and models could do at the expense of realizing what they could not do (there has always been a tendency since the 1980s to attempt to transform economics into an exact science, while it will always remain a social science). In the frenzy to drive revenue models, the downside was so eclipsed by the upside that institutions, rating agencies, and regulators neglected to focus on or even ask about the downside. The so-called sophistication of these quantitative models has distracted people from remembering what models can and cannot do. In many cases, people could not even comprehend these limitations. Models often are meant to convey one thing through resemblance, but due to the lack of an understanding of the full picture, their meaning can become something else.

Interestingly, the answer to sophistication and complexity is de facto simplicity. Risk management is based on the theory of probability and thus has an implied assumption that events can be predicted. Therefore, effective decision making that relies on data mining, such as today in risk management, requires turning complexities into simpler inputs. Even with modern quantitative models that pretend to have an ability to predict all events with up to 99 percent or higher probabilities, they always rely on assumptions. While unknown uncertainty cannot be quantified, it can be effectively managed through an a priori contrarian approach; applying complex decision rules in a complex environment is a recipe for disaster.

Lending has been around for many centuries, and unfortunately, there have been financial failures regularly. However, except for cases of financial misconduct or fraud, these failures have typically been caused by problems with tail risks. In today's world, large financial firms derive a much larger proportion of their revenues from market risk instead of from credit activities, thereby changing the magnitude and severity of tail risks particularly. On one hand, today, risks can be transferred through securitization and CDS, for instance. On the other hand, the world has become much more interconnected and global. Market risk policies also require the robustness and objectivity of credit policies to shield the firm from extreme financial market risks.

MUTUALIZING RISK RESOURCES WITH FINANCE

Currently, for big data and a multitude of required regulatory reporting, it is essential that, within organizations (e.g., financial institutions and firms), staff from the risk management team work closely together with the finance team. In other words, the team falling under the CRO must exchange information with the team falling under the CFO and vice versa. Particularly, when assessing the various IT platforms used to measure risk exposures, loan loss provisions, economic capital, and so on, it is a prerequisite that the data used by the risk management department is the same as the data used by the finance department. To that effect, it is paramount to have people from the finance department attend key risk committees to validate the information used by risk managers. Risk management is also a question of information management.

Thus, to remain informed and involved in risk management activities, managers must "be able to better understand, manage, and analyze the various risk exposures. With more organizations having to work with fewer resources and lower budgets, gathering and maintaining this information"[144] can be an overwhelming and time-consuming process. As such, a robust (tail) risk management system requires an efficient risk management information system that allows businesses to readily cross-examine aggregated data and understand the true cost of risk.

RESILIENT BUSINESS MODEL

There is a need for a crucial shift in the regulatory and risk management philosophies toward looking at systemic risks and the resiliency of business models rather than assuming all risks can be identified and managed at the level of the individual firm. Unfortunately, however, even if these proposed solutions are upheld, they will remain incomplete as long as merely mechanics are emphasized and not the people.

Therefore, how do we cope with this false sense of certainty? The answer is simple. We should try to create institutions that will not fall apart when they encounter black swans. "To create strong institutions, the focus needs to shift from event definition to damage definition or to a damage-centric approach."[145] By addressing the maximum potential damage or extreme tail risk, regardless of the event that causes the damage, banks can ensure they will not fall apart in crises. This is not easy today, as there is no damage-centric metric for extreme risk. Bear Stearns and Lehman Brothers did not just have too much extreme tail risk; they also did not know how close to the precipice they were operating. Such a metric is needed to address extreme tail risk from unknown unknowns.

---

144 "Risk Management Information System (RMIS)," ajg.com, https://www.ajg.com/media/1698584/risk-management-information-system-rmis.pdf.

145 P. Karamjeet, "What Stress Testing Is Not," *Forbes*, 2014, https://www.forbes.com/sites/realspin/2014/09/22/what-stress-testing-is-not/.

FORECASTING TAIL RISKS

Tail risk management has mostly been the focus of important theoretical literature that aims at explaining how real aggregate tail risks can arise from a variety of shock configurations at disaggregated levels of an economy and how one can model and hedge against them. However, while some tail risks can be prevented, as many find their sources in complacency and reckless strategic behavior, I prefer not to spend too much time in forecasting tail risks.

The recent GFC and its hostile effects on the real economy have fueled renewed efforts in attempting to measure and monitor adverse tail events in both the financial and corporate sectors. Many methods do exist, but most focus exclusively on vulnerabilities in the financial system or some of its components with no assessment of either the impact on real activity or how vulnerabilities in the real sector may affect the financial sector.

GEOFINANCE, GEOPOLITICS, AND FINANCIAL MARKETS

The combination of geopolitics with financial markets remains a strong determinant of future actions. Tail risks in relation to geofinance are a hot topic; the tandem "tail-risks-plus-geofinance" is really a fashionable topic today. However, tail risks and geofinance are also complicated; by asset type, by industry, by risk type, by business, by region, and by just about every other metric, tail risks keep getting more and more complicated when put into relation to geofinance.

Spotting future financial industrial trading-market trends and political events can be difficult to quantify, particularly fat-tail events. However, without any doubt, they count. Market participants today cannot afford to step into the world without having made sense of phenomena that might not be expressed in numbers. In the years following the end of the Cold War, market participants focused primarily on "normalized" macroeconomic trends when attempting to determine financial market outcomes. Black swan market events, and even geofinancial and country risks, were treated as an afterthought, a mere blip on the radar screen.

Prior to the Eurozone crisis, very few had predicted that the countries of South Europe would fall into financial disarray, or that Brexit would ever take place. Most companies, be it financial institutions, corporations, or government agencies, did not allocate meaningful resources to fat TRM, and they lacked the vision to adopt a holistic approach that would embed, for instance, country and geopolitical risk into an investment and lending process.

Now, however, geopolitics and country risks are a much more potent force that can undermine the global financial market; not only can fat-tail events shape the economic environment and fundamental investment outlook, driving economic growth and asset returns, but they can potentially blindside an investment portfolio.

In this environment, understanding fat-tail geofinancial risk is important for determining outcomes for the economy and financial markets. The type of geofinancial event can determine how financial markets behave and whether the reaction is temporary or sustained, local or global. However, since probability, causality, timing, magnitude, and impact are difficult to assess, market participants rarely give geofinance the full attention it deserves.

TAIL RISKS FOR 2017

Tail risks below the radar:

- Euro debt and bank crisis
- European Union breakup
- US unwinding of the Federal Reserve Bank balance sheet and interest rate hike
- US presidency and rise of global populism (North America, Europe, Asia)
- A second Cold War between the West and Russia/China
- The oil price slump and impact on the US oil industry
- Middle East and nuclear arms race

- Middle East—the redrawing of maps (Syria, Iraq, Yemen, Libya, and Lebanon)
- Chinese economy's hard landing
- Japan's refinancing risk
- Emerging market currency crisis
- Confrontation with China in the South China Sea and East China Sea

Acknowledgments

I wish to thank my wife, Barbara, for her unwavering support throughout the process of writing this book: her love and advice have kept me going throughout all these years.

I also thank numerous former colleagues, among which Massimo Piras, as well as academici from for providing insightful comments on the content and flow of this book.

Bibliography

The literature on extreme risk is vast. The bibliography of works covering various aspects is not intended to be exhaustive or comprehensive, but many of the following books, articles, research papers, websites, and conferences allowed for the drafting of this book.

Aboura, S. *Disentangling Crashes from Tail Events*. Paris: Universite de Paris Dauphine, 2012.

Akoundi, K. *Tail Risk Hedging: A Roadmap for Asset Owners*. New York: Deutsche Bank, 2010.

Bari, A. *Predictive Analytics*. Hoboken, NJ: John Wiley & Sons, 2014.

Blackwill, R. *War by Other Means, Geoeconomics and Statecraft*. Cambridge, MA: Harvard University Press, 2016.

Boin, A., *Designing Resilience: Preparing for Extreme Events*, Pittsburgh, PA, University of Pittsburgh Press, 2010.

Castillo, C. *Big Crisis Data, Social Media in Disasters and Time-Critical Situations*. Cambridge: Cambridge University Press, 2016.

Chava, S. *Do Bond Investors Price Tail Risk Exposures of Financial Institutions?* Houston, TX: Bauer College of Business, University of Houston, 2014.

Clauset, A. *A Brief Primer on Probability Distributions*. Santa Fe, NM: Santa Fe Institute, 2011.

Comfort, L. K. *Designing Resilience*. Pittsburgh, PA: University of Pittsburgh Press, 2010.

Copeland, D. C. *Economic Interdependence and War*. Princeton, NJ: Princeton University Press, 2015.

Diebold, F. *The Known, the Unknown, and the Unknowable in Financial Risk Management*. Princeton, NJ: Princeton University Press, 2010.

El-Erian, M. *The Only Game in Town, Central Banks, Instability, and Avoiding the Next Collapse*. New York: Random House, 2016.

El-Erian, M. *When Markets Collide, Investment Strategies for the Age of Global Economic Change*. New York: McGraw Hill, 2008.

Embrechts, P., C. Klüppelberg, and T. Mikosch. *Modelling Extremal Events: For Insurance and Finance*. New York: Springer, 2008.

Empiricus, S., trans., and Loeb Robert Gregg Bury, ed. *Outlines of Pyrrhonism*. London: W. Heinemann, 1933.

Ewan Rankin, M. S. *A Century of Stock Bond Correlations*. Canberra: Reserve Bank of Australia Bulletin, 2014.

Federal Reserve Bank of St Louis, Economic Research, Board of the Governors of the Federal Reserve System.

Fingar, T. *Reducing Uncertainty, Intelligence and Natinal Security.* Stanford, CA: Stanford University Press, 2011.

Galbraith, J. K. *The End of Normal: The Great Crisis and the Future of Growth.* New York: Simon & Schuster, 2014.

Goldfinger, C. *La Geofinance, Pour Comprendre la Mutation Financiere.* Paris: Seuil, 1986.

Greenspan, A. *The Map and the Terrirory, Risk, Human Nature, and the Future of Forecasting.* New York: The Penguin Press, 2013.

Haitao Li, Z. S. *Tail Risk in Fixed Income Markets.* Beijing: Cheung Kong Graduate School of Business, 2015.

Hume, D. *Enquiries concerning Human Understanding and concerning the Principles of Morals.* Oxford: Clarendon Press, 1777.

Ivantsov, E. *Heads or Tail, Financial Disaster, Risk Management and Survival Strategy in Extreme Risk.* Abingdon-on-Thames: Routledge, 2013.

Karamjeet, P. *Managing Extreme Financial Risk: Strategies and Tactics for Going Concerns.* Amsterdam: Elsevier, 2014.

Keat, I. B. *The Fat Tail: The Power of Political Knowledge for Strategic Investing.* Oxford: Oxford University Press, 2009.

Khan, O. *Managing the Supply Chain in an Age of Uncertainty.* Bedford: Cranfield School of Management, 2015.

Knaup, K. *Forward Looking Tail Risk Exposures at U.S. Bank Holding Companies.* Arlington, TX: Tilburg University, 2012.

Knaup, M. *Measuring the Tail Risk of Banks*. Arlington, TX: Tilburg University, 2010.

Knight, F. H. *Risk, Uncertainty and Profit*. Boston, MA: Houghton Mifflin, 1921.

Kotz, S. *Extreme Value Distributions, Theory and Applications*. Nottingham: The University of Nottingham, 2000.

Lian, C. *Extreme Risk Analysis of Dynamic Interdependent Systems*. Saarbrücken: VDM Verlag Dr. Müller, 2008.

Longin, F. *Extreme Events in Finance: A Handbook of Extreme Value Theory and Its Applications*. Chicago, IL: Wiley, 2017.

Mbuya, J. C. *Enterprise Wide Holistic Risk Management*. Saarbrucken: LAP Lambert Academic Publishing, 2010.

McKay, S., *Risk assessment for mid-sized companies: Tools for Developing a Tailored Approach to Risk Management*, Durham, NC: AICPA, 2011.

McGinn, J. *Tail Risk Killers, How Math, Indeterminacy, and Hubris Distor Markets*. New York: McGraw Hills, 2012.

Nordhaus, W. *Elementary Statistics of Tail Events*. New Haven, CT: Yale University, 2011.

Novak, S. Y. *Extreme Value Methods with Applications to Finance*. London: Chapham & Hall, 2011.

O'Neil, C. *Weapons of Math Destruction, How Big Data Increases Inequality and Threatens Democracy*. New York: Crown, 2016.

Orlov, D. *The Five Stages of Collapse: Survivors' Toolkit*. Vancouver: New Society Publishers, 2013.

Pisano, G. *You Need an Innovation Strategy*. Watertown, NY: Harvard Business Review, 2015.

Popper, K. *The Logic of Scientific Discovery*. London: Hutchinson & Co., 1959.

Ray, C. *Extreme Risk Management: Revolutionary Approaches to Evaluating and Measuring Risk*. New York: McGraw-Hill Education, 2010.

Renfroe, N. *Threat, Vulnerability Assessments and Risk Analysis*. Washington, DC: Applied Research Associates Inc., 2016.

Roubini, N. *Crisis Economics, a Crash Course in the Future of Finance*. New York: Penguin Books, 2010.

Shiller, R. J. *Irrational Exuberance*. Princeton, NJ: Princeton University Press, 2015.

Silver, N. *The Signal and the Noise, Why So Many Predictions Fail—But Some Don't*. New York: The Penguin Press, 2012.

Sornette, D. *Extreme Financial Risk: From Dependence to Risk*. New York: Springer, 2006.

Swedroe, L. *Reducing the Risk of Black Swans: Using the Science to Capture Returns with Less Volatilities*. St. Louis, MO: Bam Alliance Press, 2014.

Taleb, N. N. *Antifragile, Things That Gain from Disorder.* New York: Random House, 2012.

Taleb, N. N. *The Black Swan: The Impact of the Highly Improbable*. New York: Pantheon Books, 2008.

Tapiero, C. S. *Enineering Risk and Finance*. New York: Springer, 2013.

Tetlock, Ph. *Superforecasting, the Art and Science of Prediction*. New York: Crown Publishers, 2015.

Vinals, J. *Macro Financial Stress Testing—Principles and Practices.* Washington, DC: International Monetary Fund., 2015.

Wallison, P. J. *Hidden in Plain Sight, What Really Caused the World's Worst Financial Crisis and Why It Could Happen Again*. New York: Encounter Books, 2015.

Wildavsky, A. *Searching for Safety.* Piscataway, NJ: Studies in Social Philosophy Policy, Transaction Publishers, 1988.

Wolf, M. *De Shifts en de Shocks*. Houten: Spectrum, 2014.

Zolli, A. M. *Resilience Why Things Bounce Back*. New York: Simon & Schuster, 2013.

Works Cited

Akoundi, K. 2012. *Tail Risk Hedging: A Roadmap for Asset Owners*. New York: Deutsche Bank.

Allianz. 2015. "Allianz Global Investors Risk Monitor." *Edition 2015.*

Armoghan, M. 2011. "Black Swans Turn Grey: The Transformation of Risk." PwC, http://pwc.blogs.com/files/black-swans-turn-grey-risk-practices---the-transformation-of-risk.pdf.

Asay, M. 2013. "Blinded by Big Data: It's the Models, Stupid." ReadWrite, http://readwrite.com/2013/05/20/blinded-by-big-data/.

Asness, C. 2001. "Do Hedge Funds Hedge?" *The Journal of Portfolio Management* 28:6–19.

Bank of International Settlements, B. F. 2005. *Stress Testing at Major Financial Institutions: Survey Results and Practice.* Basel: Working Group Report Committee on the Global Financial System.

Beattie, J. 2014. "Did You Know Your Business Continuity Plan Can Help with your Company's Living Will." *Forbes.* https://www.forbes.com/sites/

sungardas/2014/02/24/did-you-know-your-business-continuity-plan-can-help-with-your-companys-living-will/#2b288614406c.

Benson, R., R. K. Shapiro, D. Smith, and R. Thomas. 2011. "A Comparison of Tail Risk Protection Strategies in the U.S. Market." *Alternative Investment Analyst Review.* https://www.caia.org/sites/default/files/2013-aiar-q1-comparison.pdf.

Bhansali, V. 2008. "Tail Risk Management: Why Investors Should Be Chasing Their Tails." *Pimco*, December.

Bilich, T. 2014. "What Risk Management is Not," Risk Alternatives. http://risk-alternatives.com/what-risk-management-is-not/.

Booz & Co, 2017. "A Comprehensive Risk Appetite Framework for Banks." PWC. Accessed May 4, 2017. https://www.strategyand.pwc.com/media/file/Risk_Appetite_Framework.pdf.

Cecchetti, S. 2010. "Toward a Global Risk Map." BIS Working Paper No 309. Basel: Bank for International Settlements.

Cecchetti, S. 2015. "The Mythic Quest for Early Warnings—Money, Banking and Financial." Money and Banking. http://www.moneyandbanking.com/commentary/2015/4/13/the-mythic-quest-for-early-warnings.

Chee, J. 2015. "Tail Risk Management Strategies," Willis Towers WatsonCulp, S. 2012. "Political Risk Can't Be Avoided, But It Can Be Managed." *Forbes*, August 2.

Connor, M. 2014. "Education Series Understanding Tail Risk," Pimco, July, https://www.pimco.com/en-us/resources/education/understanding-tail-risk/.

Durden, T. 2014. "The Annotated History of Global Volatility." *ZeroHedge*, June 26.

Eisen, B. 2013. "So What Does a Shrinking Swap Spread Mean Anyway?" MarketWatch. http://blogs.marketwatch.com/thetell/2013/12/18/so-what-does-a-shrinking-swap-sp.

Feliciano, J., 2017. "The Risk Management of Product Design." Intercompany Long Term Care Insurance. http://iltciconf.org/index_htm_files/44-Risk%20Mgmt%20session.pdf.

Fiksel, J., 2015. "From Risk to Resilience: Learning to Deal With Disruption." MIT Sloan Management Review & Report. http://tribunecontentagency.com/article/from-risk-to-resilience-learning-to-deal.

Forest, A. 2016. "Effective Downside Risk Management." Schroders Global Ft.com/lexicon, 2017, http://www.schroders.com/en/sysglobal-assets/digital/expert-magazine/pdfs/sro_expert-19_3_2016_en.pdf; "Financial Times Lexicon Fat Tails." *The Financial Times*, accessed May 4, 2017, http://lexicon.ft.com/Term?term=fat-tails.

Gerstein, A. 2012. "The Challenges in Hedging Tail Risk." *The New York Times*, April 20.

Goel, A. 2016. "How Can RegTechs Help Financial Services Industry Overcome the Burden of Compliance?" Let's Talk Payments. Last Modified May 9, 2016. https://letstalkpayments.com/how-can-regtechs-help-financial-services-industry-overcome-the-burden-of-compliance/.

Gorton, D. 2015. "Aspects of Modeling Fraud Prevention of Online Financial Services." Doctoral thesis, KTH Royal Institute of Technology, Stockholm, Sweden.

Gotz, M. 2016. "Engaging Risk: Creating a Risk-Aware Culture." EY. http://www.ey.com/Publication/vwLUAssets/EY-engaging-risk-creating-a-risk-aware-culture-through-a-more-engaging-GRC-user-experience/$File/EY-engaging-risk-creating-a-risk-aware-culture-through-a-more-engaging-GRC-user-experience.pdf.

Harris, K. 2012. "Resilience: A Risk Management Approach." Overseas Development Institute GFDRR. http://www.gfdrr.org/sites/gfdrr.org/files/ODI.pdf.

Jain, S. 2014. "Why Leading Indicators and the Default Rate Help Predict." Yahoo Finance. http://finance.yahoo.com/news/why-leading-indicators-default-rate-192404433.html.

Karamjeet, P. 2013. "Time to Grab Extreme Risk by the Tail." *American Banker*, November 8.

Karamjeet, P. 2014. "Boards Must Make Extreme Risk A Priority." *Agenda, A Financial Times Service*, February 10.

Karamjeet, P. 2014. "What Stress Testing Is Not." *Forbes*, September 22. https://www.forbes.com/sites/realspin/2014/09/22/what-stress-testing-is-not/

Karamjeet, P. 2016. "Surviving the Next Crisis." *Money&Markets*, January 6.

Keller, C. 2013. "Tail Risk." Gen Re Publications.

Kenealy, B. 2014. "Risk Managers Advised to Focus on Building Resilient Firms." Business Insurance. http://www.businessinsurance.com/article/20140330/NEWS06/303309970/1235.

Knowledge@Wharton, E. L. 2015. *Global Banking 2020: Foresights & Insights*. Philadelphia, PA: EY and the Wharton School.

Kotz, S., and S. Nadarajah. 2000. *Extreme Value Distributions, Theory and Applications*. Singapore: World Scientific.

Leigh, D. 2015. "What's in Your Profile." DefCon Cyber Enterprise Cybersecurity Risk Management. https://rofori.wordpress.com/tag/nist-cybersecurity-framework/.

Li, Y. 2016, "Institutional Herding and Its Price Impact: Evidence from the Corporate Bond Market" Federal Reserve Board, Washington D.C. 2016-091

Lohrey, J., 2014 "How to Calculate Probable Maximum Loss," eHow,

Lundstrom, S. 2014. "IDC FutureScape: Worldwide Financial Services 2015 Predictions." *IDC Research*.

Madiallo, H. 2016 "Strategic Management Plan Flashcards," Quizlet, https://quizlet.com/52254636/strategic-management-plan-flash-cards/.

Marks, N., 2014. "Misunderstanding Risk and Controls." Ia Online Home. https://iaonline.theiia.org/misunderstanding-risk-and-controls.

Marsh, J., 2012 "Risk managers unprepared for flock of black swans," The Actuary Newsdesk, January 17, 2012.

Martin, D., 2012, "Basel III Challenges, Impact and Consequences, March 2012," EY Global Regulatory Network, , https://www.eycom.ch/en/Publications/20120323-Basel-3-challenges-impact-and-consequences/download.

McCormick, L. C. 2014. "U.S. 2-Year Swap Spread Reaches Widest in a Year as Stocks." Bloomberg. https://www.bloomberg.com/news/articles/2014-08-08/u-s-2-year-swap-spread-reaches-widest-in-a-year-as-stocks-drop.

McGrane V. 2014. "Fed to Hit Bog Banks with Stiffer Surcharge." *Wall Street Journal*, September 9.

Melnyk, S. 2011. "Understanding Supply Chain Resilience." Supply Chain 24/7, Dept. of Supply Chain Management, Michigan State University. http://www.supplychain247.com/article/understanding_supply_chain_resilience.

Meyer, A. 2014. "Planning for Profitability." *Banking Technology*. Sunguard.

Mitchell, T. 2012. "Resilience: A Risk Management Approach." Overseas Development Institute. https://www.odi.org/resources/docs/7552.pdf.

Moore, C. 2015. "Geopolitical Risk—The Fear and Reality for Financial Markets" Columbia Threadneedle Investments. https://www.columbiathreadneedleus.com/content/columbia/pdf/GEOPOLITICAL.PDF.

Nassim, N., and D. G. Taleb. 2009. "The Six Mistakes Executives Make in Risk Management." *Harvard Business Review*, October.

National Institute of Standards and Technology, N. I. 2012. *Guide for Conducting Risk Assessments*. Washington, DC: US Department of Commerce.

Neumann, M. 2012. "Risk Appetite: Linkage Between Risk Appetite and Strategic Planning." Washington DC ERM Symposium. April

Newhouse, J. 1982. "A Reporter at Large: A Sporty Game: 1-Betting the Company." *The New Yorker*, June 14, 48–105.

Pazderka, B. 2014 "Threat vs Vulnerability vs Risk: What Is the Difference?," Pinkterton, October 16.

Park, J. 2013. "Integrating Risk and Resilience Approaches to Catastrophe." Society for Risk Analysis. https://asu.pure.elsevier.com/en/publications/integrating-risk-and-resilience-ap.

Patel, S. 2014. "Vendor Assurance," CloudeAssurance, https://www.cloudeassurance.com/services/vendor-assurance/.

Peterson, G. 2012. *Applying Resilience Thinking, Seven Principles for Building Resilience in Social Ecological Systems*. Stockholm: Stockholm University.

Phipps, M. 2016. "What Are Correlated and Non-Correlated Assets?" The Balance. https://www.thebalance.com/what-is-asset-correlation-2894312.

Pisano, G. 2015. *You Need an Innovation Strategy*. Watertown, NY: Harvard Business Review.

Rankin, E. 2014. *A Century of Stock Bond Correlations*. Canberra: Reserve Bank of Australia Bulletin.

Ribiero, J. 2010. "Global Risk Management Survey: Sixth Edition Risk—Risk Management in the Spotlight." Deloitte. http://www.ucop.edu/enterprise-risk-management/_files/deloitte_globalrskmgtsrvy.pdf.

Risk Management Events. 2013. "Effective Tail Risk Management versus Excessive Protection." RME, PRMIA. https://prmiadc.wordpress.com/themes/governance/effective-tail-risk-management-v.

RiskMonitor Asia-Pacific Edition, 2016," allianzgi.hk, https://www.allianzgi.hk/en/downloads/others/al5agi-risk-monitor-2016-ap-version

Roubini, N., 2015. "China Shows Investors Need a Better Financial Early." MarketWatch. http://www.marketwatch.com/story/china-shows-investors-need-a-better-financial-early-warning-system-2015-08-27.

Ryan, M. 2015 "A Car and Brakes: Risk Management Is Not Risk Avoidance," The BRT Blog, March 27.

Saini, D. S. 2014. "Does Scenarios Planning Help in Strategic Risk Management." Research Gate. https://www.researchgate.net/post/Does_Scenarios_Planning_Help_In_Strategic_Risk_Management.

Shang, K. 2012. "Risk Appetite: Linkage with Strategic Planning." Society of Actuaries. http://www.actuarialpost.co.uk/article/risk-appetite:--linkage-with-strategic-pl.

Silver, N. 2012. *The Signal and the Noise, Why So Many Predictions Fail—But Some Don't.* New York: The Penguin Press.

Simchi-Levi, D. 2014. "From Superstorms to Factory Fires: Managing Unpredictable." *Harvard Business Review.* https://hbr.org/2014/01/from-superstorms-to-factory-fires-managing-unpredictable-supply-chain-disruptions.

Simchi-Levi, D. 2015. *Find the Weak Link in your Supply Chain.* Watertown: Harvard Business Review.

SSGA. 2015. "Equity Market Risk: Getting The Big One Right." State Street Global Advisors. https://www.ssga.com/investment-topics/equity/gmo-2015-equity-market-risk-getting-the-big-one-right.pdf.

Stokes, D., 2012, "Energy Risk Management: The Demise of Value at Risk," Timera Energy, March 19.

Strischek, D. 2014. "Revenue Projections with a Learning Curve." *Construction Executive Risk Management*.

Swedroe, L. 2009. "Correlation of Returns: The Reason Why Diversification Didn't Work." Moolanomy. http://www.moolanomy.com/1345/correlation-of-returns-the-reason-why-diversificat.

Taleb, N. N. 2007. "The Black Swan: Chapter 1: The Impact of the Highly Improbable." *The New York Times,* April 22, 1.

The Institute of internal Auditors. 2013. "The Three Lines of Defense in Effective Risk Management and Control." *IIA Position Paper,* January.

Webster, W. 2010 "Governance & Regulation," Barbican Consulting, August 20, 2010.

Zavatsky, D. 2013. "Complaceny: The Greatest Risk of All." *Food Safety News*.

Glossary

- Anti–money laundering (AML): a set of rules and regulations aimed at prohibiting corporations from generating income through illegal actions.
- Basel III: a wide-ranging set of financial reform measures, developed in 2010–2011 by the Swiss-based Basel Committee on Banking Supervision, to reinforce the regulation, supervision, and risk management of the banking sector in particular. The predecessors to Basel III were Basel II (2004) and Basel I (1988).
- Big data: very large data sets that may be analyzed by means of large processors to disclose patterns, trends, and associations, especially relating to human behavior and interactions.
- Black swan: an event or occurrence that diverges beyond what is normally expected of a situation and is extremely hard to forecast. The term was popularized by Nassim Nicholas Taleb, a finance professor, writer, risk analyst, and former Wall Street trader. Black swan events are typically random and are unexpected. (See also gray swan.)
- Bond: a debt security in which an investor loans money to an entity (typically corporate or governmental), which borrows the funds for a defined period of time at a variable or fixed interest rate.
- Business continuity planning (BCP): a strategy through the recognition of operational threats and risks facing a company, with an

eye on ensuring that personnel and assets are protected and able to function in the event of a disaster.

- Business resiliency: the ability of an organization to quickly adapt to disruptions while maintaining continuous business operations and safeguarding people, assets, and overall brand equity.
- Clawback provision: a particular contractual clause typically included in employment contracts by financial firms, by which money already paid must be paid back under certain conditions.
- Collateralized debt obligation (CDO): a structured asset-backed security whereby pooled assets—such as mortgages, bonds, and loans—are essentially debt obligations that serve as collateral for the CDO. The tranches in a CDO vary substantially in their risk profile.
- Commodity: a basic good used in commerce that is interchangeable with other commodities of the same type; commodities are most often used as inputs in the production of other goods or services, such as iron and coal.
- Concentration risk: a banking term denoting the overall spread of a bank's outstanding accounts over the number or variety of debtors to whom the bank has lent money. This risk is calculated using a "concentration ratio," which explains what percentage of the outstanding accounts each bank loan represents.
- Conditional value at risk (CoVaR; also called expected shortfall [ES], average value at risk [AVaR], or expected tail loss [ETL]): estimates the risk of an investment in a conservative way, focusing on the less profitable outcomes.
- Correlation: a statistical technique that can show whether and how strongly pairs of variables are related.
- Counterparty risk: the risk to each party of a contract that the counterparty will not live up to its contractual obligations. Counterparty risk is a risk to both parties and should be considered when evaluating a contract. In most financial contracts, counterparty risk is also known as default risk.

- Crash: a sudden, dramatic decline of stock prices across a significant cross-section of a stock market, resulting in a significant loss of paper wealth. Crashes are driven by panic as much as by underlying economic factors. They often follow speculative stock market bubbles.
- CRD IV: on July 17, 2013, the CRD IV package was transposed—via a regulation (Regulation [EU] No 575/2013 on prudential requirements for credit institutions and investment firms [CRR]) and a directive (Directive 2013/36/EU on access to the activity of credit institutions and the prudential supervision of credit institutions).
- Credit default swap (CDS): a financial contract whereby a buyer of corporate or sovereign debt in the form of bonds attempts to eliminate possible loss arising from default by the issuer of the bonds. This is achieved by the issuer of the bonds insuring the buyer's potential losses as part of the agreement.
- Credit risk: the risk of default on a debt that may arise from a borrower failing to make required payments. In the first resort, the risk is that of the lender and includes lost principal and interest, disruption to cash flows, and increased collection costs.
- Credit spread: the difference in yield between two bonds of similar maturity but different credit quality.
- Crisis: any event that is, or is expected to lead to, an unstable and dangerous situation affecting an individual, group, community, or whole society.
- Default rate: the rate of borrowers who fail to remain current on their loans. This is a critical piece of information used by lenders to determine their risk exposure and by economists to evaluate the health of the overall economy.
- Derivative: a contract between two or more parties based on the asset or assets. Its value is determined by fluctuations in the underlying asset. The most common underlying assets include stocks, bonds, commodities, currencies, interest rates, and market indexes.

- Diversification: the process of allocating capital in a way that reduces the exposure to any one particular asset or risk.
- Dodd-Frank Wall Street Reform and Consumer Protection Act: a massive piece of financial reform legislation passed by the Obama administration in 2010 as a response to the financial crisis of 2008.
- Early-warning system (EWS): helps risk managers identify and communicate emerging systemic risks.
- Economic capital: the amount of risk capital, assessed on a realistic basis, that a firm requires to cover the risks that it is running or collecting as a going concern, such as market risk, credit risk, legal risk, and operational risk.
- Emerging risks: new and unforeseen risks whose potential for harm or loss is not fully known.
- Enterprise risk management (ERM): encompasses all risks across an enterprise, both pure and speculative.
- European Markets and Infrastructure Regulation (EMIR): a European Union law that aims to reduce the risks posed to the financial system by derivatives transactions. It impacts European and non-European financial institutions and corporates.
- Exotic collateralized debt obligation: a complex CDO using exotic financial instruments, usually derivatives that are more complex than commonly traded "vanilla" products. The category may also include derivatives with a nonstandard subject matter (i.e., underlying), developed for a particular client or a particular market.
- Expected default frequency (EDF): a measure of the probability that a firm will default over a specified period of time (typically one year). "Default" is defined as failure to make scheduled principal or interest payments.
- Expected loss (EL): the loss that can be incurred as a result of lending to a company that may default. It is the average loss in value over a specified period.
- Exposure at default (EAD): the total value that a bank is exposed to at the time of a loan's default. Exposure at default, along with

loss given default (LGD) and probability of default (PD), is used to calculate the credit risk capital of financial institutions.

- Extract, transform, load (ETL): refers to a process in database usage and especially in data warehousing.
- Extreme risks: risks of very bad outcomes or "high consequence" but of low probability.
- Extreme value theory (EVT) or extreme value analysis (EVA): a branch of statistics dealing with the extreme deviations from the median of probability distributions. It seeks to assess, from a given ordered sample of a given random variable, the probability of events that are more extreme than any previously observed.
- Fat-tailed distribution: one of the so-called heavy-tailed statistical distributions that describe the probability of certain events. Fat tails have a sharp bell shape, which leads to the term *leptokurtosis*, another name for a fat-tailed distribution.
- Federal Emergency Management Agency (FEMA)
- Financial continuity/contingency planning (FCP): the creation of a strategy through the recognition of financial threats and risks facing a company, with an eye on ensuring that personnel and assets are protected and able to function in the event of a financial crisis.
- Financial risk management: the practice of economic value in a firm by using financial instruments to manage exposure to risk, operational risk, credit risk, and market risk.
- Funding risk: the risk associated with the impact on a project's cash flow from higher funding costs or lack of availability of funds.
- Gaussian distribution: also commonly called the "normal distribution," often described as a bell-shaped curve. If the probability of a single event is *p* and there are *n* events, then the value of the Gaussian distribution function at value *x* is ×10^.
- Geofinance: a method of studying financial markets to understand, explain, and predict financial behavior through geographical variables. These include area geology and physical geography, but

also human geography, in the sense of human behavior impacting financial markets and organizations.

- Geopolitics: a method of studying foreign policy to understand, explain, and predict international political behavior through geographical variables. These include area studies, climate, topography, demography, natural resources, and applied science of the region being evaluated.
- Global financial crisis (GFC): the financial crisis that took place in 2007–2008 and started in the United States.
- Gray swan: An event that can be anticipated to a certain degree but is considered unlikely to occur and may have a sizable impact on the valuation of a security or the health of the overall market if it does occur. A gray swan event is unlike a black swan event, whose total impact is difficult to predict.
- Hadoop: an open-source software framework for storing data and running applications on clusters of commodity hardware. It provides massive storage for any kind of data, enormous processing power, and the ability to handle virtually limitless concurrent tasks or jobs.
- Hedge: an investment to reduce the risk of adverse price movements in an asset. Normally, a hedge consists of taking an offsetting position in a related security, such as a futures contract.
- High-reliability organization (HRO): an organization that has succeeded in avoiding catastrophes in an environment where normal accidents can be expected due to risk factors and complexity.
- Holistic approach: relating to or concerned with wholes or with complete systems rather than with the analysis of, treatment of, or dissection into parts.
- Loss given default (LGD): the share of an asset that is lost if a borrower defaults. This is a common parameter in risk models and also a parameter used in the calculation of economic capital, expected loss, or regulatory capital under Basel II for a banking institution.

- Market risk: the possibility for an investor to experience losses due to factors that affect the overall performance of the financial markets in which he or she is involved. Market risk, also called *systematic risk*, cannot be eliminated through diversification, though it can be hedged against.
- Mathematical-financial model: a mathematical model designed to represent a simplified version of the performance of a financial asset or portfolio of a business, project, or any other investment.
- Modern portfolio theory (MPT): a theory on how risk-averse investors can construct portfolios to optimize or maximize expected return based on a given level of market risk, emphasizing that risk is an inherent part of higher reward.
- Moody's KMV: a model based on the structural approach to calculate EDF (credit risk is driven by the firm value process).
- Normal distribution: a very common continuous probability distribution. Normal (or Gaussian) distributions are important in statistics and are often used in the natural and social sciences to represent real-valued random variables whose distributions are not known.
- Operational risk: the prospect of loss resulting from inadequate or failed procedures, systems, or policies, including employee errors, systems failures, fraud or other criminal activity, and any event that disrupts business processes.
- Pareto effect: states that, for many events, roughly 80 percent of the effects come from 20 percent of the causes.
- Power law: a relationship between two quantities such that one is proportional to a fixed power of the other.
- Probability of default (PD): a financial term describing the likelihood of a default over a particular time horizon. It provides an estimate of the likelihood that a borrower will be unable to meet its debt obligations. PD is used in a variety of credit analyses and risk management frameworks.

- Probability: the measure of the chance that an event will occur as a result of an experiment.
- Probable maximum loss (PML): the maximum loss that an insurer would be expected to incur on a policy. PML is most often associated with insurance policies on property, such as fire insurance. The PML represents the worst-case scenario for an insurer.
- Regulatory capital (also known as capital requirement or capital adequacy): the amount of capital a bank or other financial institution has to hold as required by its financial regulator. This is usually expressed as a capital adequacy ratio of equity that must be held as a percentage of risk-weighted assets.
- Reverse stress testing: the process of uncovering events that, should they occur, have the potential to make your business unviable. Such events can cover credit, market, and liquidity risk. It's important to remember that business failure occurs before you run out of capital. It's when counterparties are unwilling to deal with you.
- Risk: the potential of gaining or losing something of value.
- Risk averse: disinclined or reluctant to take risks.
- Risk Exposure Index (REI): a mathematical, computerized description of supply chains developed by MIT professor David Simchi-Levi and his colleagues, used to successfully manage unpredictable supply chain disruptions.
- Risk measurement: evaluation of the likelihood and extent (magnitude) of a risk.
- Risk-weighted assets (RWA): a bank's assets or off-balance-sheet exposures, weighted according to risk. This sort of asset calculation is used in determining the capital requirement or capital adequacy ratio (CAR) for a financial institution.
- Scenario analysis: a process of analyzing possible future events by considering alternative possible outcomes (sometimes called *alternative worlds*). Scenario analysis, which is one of the main forms of projection, does not try to show one exact picture of the future.

- Skewness: a measure of the asymmetry of the probability distribution of a real-valued random variable about its mean. The skewness value can be positive or negative, or even undefined. The qualitative interpretation of the skew is complicated and unintuitive.
- Standard deviation (SD; also represented by the Greek letter ⍰ or the Latin letter *s*): a measure that is used to quantify the amount of variation or dispersion of a set of data values.
- Stock: a general term used to describe the ownership certificates of any company; *shares* refers to the ownership certificates of a particular company. So if investors say they own stocks, they are generally referring to their overall ownership in one or more companies.
- Stress testing: a form of deliberately intense or thorough testing used to determine the stability of a given system or entity. It involves testing beyond normal operational capacity, often to a breaking point, in order to observe the results.
- Supply chain risk management (SCRM): the implementation of strategies to manage both everyday and exceptional risks along the supply chain based on continuous risk assessment with the objective of reducing vulnerability and ensuring continuity.
- Tail risk management (TRM): the risk management of extreme events—black swans.
- Time to recover (TTR): the time that a device will take to recover from any failure. Examples of such devices range from self-resetting fuses (where the MTTR would be very short, probably seconds), up to whole systems that have to be repaired or replaced.
- Traditional risk management: focuses on pure risks and views each risk separately.
- Uncertainty: in metrology, physics, and engineering, the uncertainty or margin of error of a measurement, when explicitly stated, is given by a range of values likely to enclose the true value. This

may be denoted by error bars on a graph, or by the following notation: measured value ± uncertainty.

- Value at risk (VaR): a measure of the risk of investments; estimates how much a set of investments might lose, given normal market conditions, in a set time period such as a day. VaR is typically used by firms and regulators in the financial industry to gauge the amount of assets needed to cover possible losses.
- Volatility: a statistical measure of the dispersion of returns for a given security or market index. Volatility can be measured by using either the standard deviation or the variance between returns from that same security or market index.

Index

U

V

www.ingramcontent.com/pod-product-compliance
Lightning Source LLC
Chambersburg PA
CBHW061208220326
41599CB00025B/4574